WHAT DOES GOD EXPECT OF PARENTS!

Down to earth support for parents in confirming their children's faith

GW00729219

Written by Michael and Terri Quinn
in co-operation with the Armagh diocesan
Family Ministry team

Handbook for the *'Confirming Faith in the Family'* Programme

FAMILY CARING TRUST

First published 2002
entitled, 'I have a million things to do.'
by Family Caring Trust,
8 Ashtree Enterprise Park
Newry, Co. Down BT34 1BY
Tel. 028 3026 4174
(Fax. 028 3026 9077)
Website: familycaring.co.uk
Email: office@familycaring.co.uk

Completely revised edition published 2003
Printing: Universities Press (Belfast)
Illustrations: Pauline McGrath, Helena Good

The Scripture quotations contained herein are
from the New Revised Standard Version Bible,
Catholic Edition, copyright © 1989 by the
Division of Christian Education of the
National Council of the Churches of Christ in the USA,
and are used by permission. All rights reserved.

Reproduction 'Supper at Emmaus
with Kitchen Maid' courtesy of the
National Gallery of Ireland.

We are grateful to Veritas Publications
for permission to include prayers from
the Alive-O school programme.

ISBN 1 872253 20 2

CONTENTS

Before You Begin...

Terri and I have taken our five children and some foster-children through Confirmation. Year after year we sat through school meetings. The teachers and priests who spoke to us were doing their best. They told us about the school programme and asked us to help our children with it. Parents around us looked at their watches. The speakers thanked us for handing on our faith and praying with our children. The parents stirred uncomfortably in their seats and put their heads down: some of them were not sure if they even *had* much faith to pass on – and family prayer was an uphill battle that most of them had given up on. They went home feeling guilty and discouraged, wanting to leave 'handing on faith' to the teachers who seemed to know a lot more about it. What they did not realise was that these good, well-meaning speakers were offering something that was not suitable for parents. Hopefully this little book will help to right the balance.

Questions and Confusion
The first thing that has to be said is that life has changed hugely since we were children. It is not all change for the worse, but parents often feel a bit lost today. Rebellious and rude behaviour is more common – and at a younger age. There are more pressures than ever. We are constantly on the run, trying to catch up. We keep going, doing our best but feeling pulled in different directions. We have little time to stop and think or ask what life is all about. Worries about our children's faith are just an additional pressure, adding to our sense of guilt and of not being able to measure up.

In writing this book, we do not pretend to have answers. We just want to offer you a chance to pause and think about what you want for yourself and your family. A book will not sort everything out, but it may help to give you a better sense of direction. Remember too: all the confusion and all the questions you have are not a bad thing – people *need* to be asking questions when they are trying to make sense of life today and to find God somewhere in the confusion!

Who is this book aimed at?
You can be sure about one thing – the answers *you* find to your questions will not be the same as other people's answers, for families come in all shapes and sizes and are in different situations. For this reason there are many things in this book that may not suit you at present but may suit some people at different stages in their journey. Use what helps you, and put aside any guilt you may have about ignoring whatever you do not find helpful.

Where do the ideas come from?
The information about parenting in these pages is based on much recent research (see www.familycaring.co.uk) which usually makes a lot of sense to parents. Our emphasis on the holiness of daily family living, however, may be different to what some of you picked up as children. It is part of the teaching of the Second Vatican Council in the 1960s, but it is only now beginning to filter through to families. Initially, some people may see it as a 'watering down of religion' because they are more comfortable with a religion of rules. But we hope it will take the place of unhelpful guilt and will free you and your family in all sorts of ways. That is what Jesus came on earth to do.

Part of a course
The book is part of a programme (two or three sessions) for parents of children preparing to make their Confirmation, but it should help any parent who picks it up. Just bear in mind that it is not meant to be read in one go, so you might leave a little time between reading each chapter. The leader's guide and video for the course is available separately from Family Caring Trust.

With a little adaptation, too, the ideas can be applied to other Christian churches – where family spirituality is often equally misunderstood and neglected.

Acknowledgements

A special word of thanks is due to the Armagh diocesan family
ministry team of lay people, priests, parents and teachers who gave
willingly of their time and energy in dreaming up and shaping this
entire project. Denis Bradley of Accord. Tony Hanna of the
Family of God Community. Muireann Maguire, catechist. Fr Peter
McAnenly, the Diocesan Adviser for Religious Education. Eileen
McCreesh, teacher. Fr Robert McKenna and Fr Andrew McNally,
the two Directors of Family Ministry during the span of the project.
Fergus McMorrow, the Diocesan Director of Youth Ministry.

We would also like to thank all the people who read and
commented on the book or helped to test the programme throughout
the archdiocese of Armagh and beyond: Mary Cunningham,
formerly of Barnardos, and Maureen Treanor of All Hallows, who
trained groups of facilitators; Vera Durkin, formerly Diocesan RE
Adviser to schools in Dromore; Fr Finbarr Lynch SJ; Naomi and
John Lederach; Peter Devlin; Breige O'Hare of Down and Connor
Family Ministry; Philip Leonard, formerly Northern Ireland director
of CMAC/Accord; David Thomas of the Bethany Family Institute;
and Fr Peter O'Reilly of Veritas.

Chapter 1: What does God *expect* of a parent!

Everyone was annoyed with Peter. He had stolen money for cigarettes, then told lies to try to cover up his crime and put the blame on his sister. When she told the truth about his stealing, he went looking for her and kicked her until she could hardly walk. Now he was grounded for two days and was in everyone's bad books. Worst of all, the granny whom he adored had just arrived and had been told the full story. She sent for Peter.

"Peter," she said, putting her arms around him, "my big handsome grandson! You've been having such a tough time lately. But everyone makes mistakes, and I know you've a heart of gold."

Peter choked back his tears. He knew his behaviour had been awful, but this was so typical of granny to overlook things like that and believe the best of you. Granny was granny...

That is what God is like too. Someone has said that God is a lousy parent who forgives you even before you say sorry and who has a special love for the 'lost sheep' and the 'bad eggs' among us. God has more time for those of us who are in pain than for those who sail along without a worry. We mess up our lives – and other people's lives – and we think God must be pretty disappointed and angry with us. Instead, God welcomes us with open arms and says,

"Peter, you've done better than I could have expected!" We know
we have messed up, and that we have *not* done better than *anybody*
expected. But just like granny, God cannot help being God – an
encourager who sees the best in you and believes the best of you...

What does God expect!
Parents need to hear that. When Confirmation time comes around,
we can feel guilty and bad about the level of faith in our homes. All
because we have such mistaken ideas of God – the policeman who
finds fault, the judge whom we can never satisfy, not the hen that
gathers her chicks under her wings or the welcoming father with the
twinkling eyes who loves us beyond all reason and wants to pour
the Spirit of Love into our hearts.

You see, God *understands* your circumstances – the worries you
have, the problems you are facing with a difficult child, your
frustration as a lone parent, your difficulties with money or with a
family drink problem... God does not expect the impossible.

Another thing: God certainly does not expect you to be running
to a lot of church ceremonies or saying a lot of prayers or talking a
lot of religion to your children. After all, what did Jesus ask us to
do? He said, "Love one another. By this everyone will know you
are my disciples if you have love one for another." He didn't say,
"Pray for a half an hour every day." We will not get too far without
saying some prayers, but **our deepest prayer is how we live our
daily lives and how we love one another.** Especially in our own
families. That is what holiness is all about, and what Confirmation
is all about – and it is what you are *already* doing! You sometimes
hear people say when someone dies, "He was holy – he was always
saying prayers." They are missing the point. It would make more
sense if they said, "He was holy – he loved everyone he met,
especially those in his own family." (We say *especially* them,
because they are the hardest to love!)

Gentlelove and Firmlove
But love means different things. What is this love that God wants
us to have? The following story may help to make it clearer:

9

Carol's dad is a lone parent. He is thrifty and manages quite well, but Carol is now pre-teen and her demands for money have been growing. Her Dad is very fond of her and finds it hard to say no. He decided recently, however, that it was time to talk.

"Carol," he said, "When you come looking for money, you sometimes catch me unprepared. So I've decided to give you a weekly allowance in future to let you manage your own money. But I won't be giving you any more handouts during the week."

When Carol heard how much the allowance would be, she was not happy and argued with him. Her dad explained that he only had so much money, but he also listened to her arguments and they talked some more – Carol eventually agreed to do some extra jobs to earn money at home.

Carol's dad is showing two kinds of love here – firmlove and gentlelove. Firmlove means taking a firm stand at times and helping children to become more responsible. Gentlelove is about being affectionate, encouraging, listening… There is general agreement today that a balance of these two kinds of love helps children to grow up feeling secure and knowing they are loved. Gentlelove may be more *important* than firmlove, but we cannot leave either of them out.

1. Gentlelove

Let's look at gentlelove first. It is about being flexible and warm and soft – like the granny in the first story. It is about hugging children, telling them stories, chatting with them, listening, praying together, eating together, having fun together. It means respecting children and giving them positive attention.

The best *time* to give positive attention is not when children are *demanding* it but when they are *not* expecting it. You buy them a treat when they are *not* whinging for it. Out of the blue you suggest a game of cards (or a water fight), you join them at bedtime for a chat, a story, a prayer, a hug…

Gentlelove is about being open to listening even at times that don't suit. It means getting to know the details of what's going on in our children's lives and remembering to ask about those details –

not 'How was school?' but "Well, how did your match go?" (You see, you knew about the match and you remembered to ask!) "What did your teacher say about your poem?" "Was Elaine back in school today?" "How's her Mum, by the way?" It means watching some of *their* TV programmes along with them instead of leaving them on their own to watch TV or play video games. They see and hear things differently when a parent is sitting beside them. We sometimes think we have much less to give children nowadays because their computer skills are better than ours, but what they will never stop needing is our presence, our time for them, our love.

Part of that love is being real with them. Our children need us to be ourselves, to say what we honestly feel and think and what is important to us. We need to be able to say, "I'm sorry" when we lose the bap, and to say, "I don't know" when we are not sure. In other words, to be human. **Children spend so much time today with TV or with their own age group and they do not have enough time with 'real' adults who can be themselves with them – which is what helps young people to mature.** That is the importance of spending time connecting with them.

At two o'clock my 13-year-old daughter woke me with a bad headache. She said the painkillers hadn't worked. "I don't know what to do," I said, "But if you like I'll sit on the bed beside you and put my hand on your head and pray silently for you." I wouldn't have done that only for what I'd heard about the importance of Gentlelove. After a few minutes, she put her hand on mine and said, "I love your hands." You've no idea how big that was from her because parents aren't 'cool' for thirteen-year-old girls!

Gentlelove is not soft or easy on *parents*. It is hard to spend time with children that we would rather spend at some sport, or tidying the house, or watching TV or working overtime. But isn't that what "Love one another" means? Not acting on our feelings. For my

11

family's sake I give *up* what I feel like doing. But isn't that what you are *already* doing so often? Putting yourself out for your children, even when you feel mad with them and do not feel *any* affection. You still get up in the middle of the night to attend to a child. You still hang in with an uncooperative son or daughter. You constantly make sacrifices of your time and money and energy. And that is love. So you are *already* doing a lot to confirm your children, allowing the Holy Spirit to strengthen and build them up. And you must not worry if you have no feelings of affection at times. *Feelings* of love are not the point with gentlelove – it is how we *act* that matters.

2. Firmlove

Gentlelove is more important than firmlove, but we need to balance the two. There are many parents today who give lots of gentlelove but they say their children are unmanageable. That is not surprising, for children need the security of *clear boundaries and limits* as *well* as warmth and affection. There are times when they need to hear a firm 'no' – even though they may react to it by telling you they hate you! Of course they will react and push the limits to see if you really mean what you say. Let's look at an example.

Gary has been watching a lot of TV recently and neglecting his homework. He comes in from school and announces:

"Quick. My favourite programme is just starting!"

"Okay," his mother said, "I'll record it and you can watch it as soon as you've done your homework."

"I need to watch it now!"

"When you've done your homework, I said."

His mother remained firm, and Gary quickly realised she was not about to change. He went off to his room.

It is important to be able to say 'no' without being rigid or harsh. Like Carol's dad in the earlier example, Gary's mother was firm but she stayed friendly. Notice that she did not even *say* the word 'no.'

Firmlove allows children to make their own choices – and then it lets them live with the *results* of their choices. Gary can decide *not* to do his homework. Carol can blow her weekly allowance in one day. But then they have to live with the results. That is how they learn. That is much more effective than falling back on useless methods of discipline like nagging, threatening – or even hitting. Another thing: when you allow your children to live with the results of their choices a few times, they learn that you mean what you say. Parenting gets easier then, and *they* have the limits they need.

Another area where parents can be firmer today is in training children to do household chores. Many parents of eleven or twelve-year-olds still make school lunches even though their children have been capable of making their own lunches for years! This is the first generation in history when most children have not had to work at home. They should at *least* have to clear up after themselves. It is good for young people, boys as well as girls, to have to do some of the tidying up chores in the kitchen, and to vacuum and sweep, and to start learning to cook one meal a week. If you live in a house, you need to play your part in looking after it. That is a lesson for life. Doing everything for children and overprotecting them may make *us* feel good, but it does not help *them* to become responsible.

One word of caution, though. Some parents reading this may decide that they have not been firm enough and need to change things. When that change does not happen fast, they start to nag and remind and scold. That is not firmlove. **Firmlove does not nag. Firmlove is patient and understanding, taking time to train children to do a new chore, not expecting adult standards.** It cannot be separated from gentlelove.

3. Love for yourself
There is another kind of love that children need (and that God invites us to practise) – self-love. 'Love your neighbour as yourself' makes little sense if I do *not* love my*self*! Children need parents who look after themselves. If we are overworked or depressed or drinking too much, if we do not make time for our wives/husbands/partners, if we do not take exercise, or learn to relax, or make time during the day for a snatch of prayer that helps

us to be aware of God in our lives, then the balance will hardly be there with our children either!

To keep this balance in our lives it can help to plan. If you are a couple, for example, experts suggest that you plan a weekly date – some time away from the children for an evening, even a walk in the nearest park, or a film, or a trip down to the local pub together for a drink. You may never have thought of that as something holy to do, something that God would *like* you to do, but one of the worst things for children is to have their parents at home fighting and rowing. One of the best things a couple can do for a child is to make time for one *another*.

On the other hand, if you are a *lone* parent, you might think about how you could get your mother or a godparent or someone to baby-sit and let you out now and again for a night with some friends. That is looking after yourself too. (And maybe that is part of what godparents are for!)

So. Finding a balance. Making time for each other. Taking some time out for exercise, relaxing and so on. Time to just *be*, to go for a walk or lie on in bed, or take a bath, or have a relaxed cup of tea. God *wants* that for us. That is partly why God wants us to have a weekly Sabbath day of rest! The Holy Spirit is the Spirit of Peace, and we do not give the Spirit a chance to work until we clear a little space in ourselves.

Part of clearing that space is taking time to pray to the Spirit about our families, especially when we have to make a decision about them or when we need to have a serious talk: 'Come Holy Spirit, I need your help now with this child!'

4. Faith in the home
That leads us to a fourth way of loving our children: *confirming their faith*. You see, **the Holy Spirit is not like the Lone Ranger. The Spirit works through *us*. *We* confirm our children *along* with the Spirit.** God works *through* our gentlelove and our firmlove and our care for ourselves. It is not that we have to *talk* much about God – but we do strengthen our children's faith when they know we pray and when they see God as important to us.

Now, it is true that some of us feel awkward about praying with our families. Sometimes we do not know how to start or what to say. But **if you do not know what to say, you can use silence instead. You might say, "Let's take a moment of silence to thank God for the food we're about to eat,"** and keep your head bowed for ten seconds. That is family prayer. In the same way, you might join your child at bedtime and say, "Let's take a moment to think about all the good things of today and thank God for some of them..." Then, after a short period of silence, you add, "We'll think now for a few moments about the times that we didn't love, and we can say sorry in our hearts..."

Even seeing you pray or bless yourself helps to confirm children's faith – so a child thinks, "My parents take God seriously. They have faith." That confirms them. That is how the Holy Spirit works.

We have just said that parents do not need to *talk* a lot about God. Example speaks far louder than words. If you feel more confident after a while, however, it can help to have an occasional chat with a child. When they say, "I hate going to Mass. It's boring!" it may be no harm to admit, if it is true, *"I often find it boring too. I just go because of my faith – I believe Jesus is present in a special way at Mass."* In the same way, you might help your children to feel okay in talking about their doubts. *"It's okay to have doubts about your faith. Some people even leave the church for a number of years. St Augustine is a good example – he lived and thought like a pagan for many years. But eventually he realised that he wasn't at peace, that nothing else could satisfy him."* When you speak to children like this, you make it normal and okay for them to have doubts and to be able to talk with you about them. At the same time your own faith is coming through – though it may be years later before it affects them!

Making changes
Let's sum up. We have looked at four ways of loving our children. Gentlelove. Firmlove. Loving *ourselves*. And showing clear signs of faith. But each one of us is limited in the amount of love we are

able to give. There is only so much change we can face. So maybe the best starting-place is to love and care for ourselves. Go easy on yourself, then. If you think it selfish and uncaring to take time for your own needs, you might ask yourself where that idea came from. Is it simply a wrong message you picked up from the family in which you grew up – that parents are supposed to do everything for their children? Once you realise where a wrong message came from, that can free you to act differently!

In order to act differently we may also need to *plan* change, bearing in mind that real change comes only from God. So we are not alone in planning change: the Holy Spirit is within each of us – always. All we need to do is ask, perhaps with a simple prayer like "Come, Holy Spirit... I'm finding it tough, and I don't know what to do. I need your support to keep on loving... Come, Holy Spirit."

What has all this to do with Confirmation?
In this chapter we have talked more about love in the family than about Confirmation. That is because the Spirit confirms our children *through* our love. In other words, we parents confirm our children *along* with the Spirit. Indeed, as we will see in the next chapter, the Holy Spirit does not just 'bounce' down on a child but works through the *whole* family.

I realise now that the best preparation for my child's Confirmation is to improve my parenting. That also makes so much sense to me.

LOOKING AHEAD: MAKING PLANS

You need space. Time for yourself. Every day. Too many parents are over-stretched, lose their sense of humour and warmth and fall back on tranquillisers, alcohol or some other escape because they do not take time to care for themselves. When you are relaxed you can love more naturally. Your children need you to look after yourself – and to take time out with your partner if you have one or with friends. They suffer when you neglect yourself or one another. Which of the things below do you think might help you to cope better? Or is there another way you need to care for yourself?

- **Regularly do something you enjoy** – listen to music, go for a swim, read a magazine, go to bingo/football, take a bath, get out in the fresh air for a walk – even *with* your children.
- **Talk to friends,** even on the phone – and plan to get out with them regularly. Ask them for help when you need a break.
- **When you're stressed or annoyed**, go for a brisk walk or leave the room, if possible. Before you act, take time to calm yourself and ask the Holy Spirit for guidance and strength.
- **Find skilled help** when you're feeling down – before things get worse. You might ring a Parentline (UK freephone 0808-800-2222, Irish Republic local call 1890-927277).

IF YOU HAVE A SPOUSE OR PARTNER...
- **Spend 10-20 minutes a day** listening and unwinding and catching up with each other over a cuppa.
- Each weekend **plan a weekly 'date'** – even a walk together.
- Look early for skilled help when there are difficulties – contact **Accord** in Ireland, **Marriage Care** or **Relate** in Britain.

My plans for this week are... _____

_____

- It will help to strengthen the effect of the course if you read Chapter One of your book in the next few days. The chapters are written in simple language and are quite short.

Chapter 2: Changing my idea of what's 'holy'

Late one night a little boy was crying, frightened by the darkness. His mother came into the room and spoke to him, "Don't worry, Andy," she said, "God is watching over you to keep you safe."

"I know God's here," Andy said, "but I want someone with some skin." His mother then got in beside him and cuddled him.

The mother laughed the next day when she told her friends the story. What she did not realise was that she really *was* God with skin. The Real Presence of Christ starts with our real presence to our children – being there for them! That is what it means when we say that Christ is alive *today*. He is present in us ordinary folk, in the people around us and in our families – for we are the Body of Christ on earth. And the work of the Holy Spirit (drawing us closer together in Christ) is to help us to *be* 'God with skin' to one another. This happens through Baptism, Confirmation and the weekly Eucharist, but the Spirit also expects us to *work* at being closer, more caring families.

Is it about 'me' or about 'us'?
Many of us miss that point. We find it hard to believe that the way to God is through our families. We even think we need to get *away* from our families in order to find God and 'inner peace.' But

holiness is being *like* God – who is not one individual person but *three persons in love*. We are not much of an image of God when we are 'me' centred. We are a much better image of three persons in love when we work at being a close family, a 'church of the home.'

That word 'church' may strike you as a strange word to apply to a family. But it is a very good word once we stop thinking of a church as a building and begin to think of it as a group of people who have four signs – one, holy, catholic and apostolic. So it can be helpful to look with fresh eyes at what these four words mean when we apply them to a family.

1. What does it mean to be 'one'?
Let's start with the first word – *one*. It can be hard for some of us to get used to the idea that **God wants us, not so much to be better individuals as to be one, to be closer** – "that they may be one, as you Father in me and I in you." But what does it mean for a family to be 'one'?

Recently we asked a number of parents to think of times when they had a sense of closeness or 'oneness' as a family. Here are some of the things they told us.

- *Tinkering at the car – with my son helping.*
- *Going for a walk with my husband, even though we weren't even talking at the start.*
- *Praying at bedtime.*
- *Going out as a family to a beautiful place.*
- *Making a decision to sit down and really listen to my son.*
- *Doing some things together, even homework sometimes.*
- *Wrestling on the floor for fun.*
- *Cuddled in bed chatting with my daughter (who had driven me crazy all day!)*
- *When my son told me he was being bullied, and cried with me.*
- *After a row where we cleared the air and made up.*
- *Making a photo album – or just looking at old photos together.*
- *Walking home from Mass on Christmas Eve night.*

- *Playing a game of Scrabble together.*
- *Crying with the children the time granddad died.*
- *Hanging out around the kitchen where the 'craic' is.*
- *Putting up decorations and preparing together for Christmas.*
- *Having an unhurried meal – with laughs and a good chat.*
- *When she was ill – I felt so close and realised how I loved her.*
- *Laughing together about what went wrong on the holidays.*
- *Playing football in the garden with my son.*
- *Laying my hand on my daughter to bless her as she lay asleep.*

I'm sure you could add your own list of close times. And it might be an idea to ask your children what *they* remember as special times of closeness. That can give us clues about how to create closeness in future!

Each family is different, of course. *You* have to decide what helps for *you* to be close. Certainly, **it will mean making efforts to be together *some* of the time for eating or chatting. Somehow we have to make *time* to connect with a child or a partner.** Time to 'hang loose' around the kitchen and have a laugh together. Time to have a serious talk when you or somebody else *needs* to talk. Time to go to children's games (especially when a child is *not* doing well!) Time to *think* about one another and *pray* for one another – what is sometimes called 'carrying one another in our hearts.'

It's the effort that counts!
That said, being close also means respecting differences. A family does not have to think the same, or do things together all the time. We must not be so close and dependent on each other that we cannot move out on our own. Closeness does not mean we cannot disagree – some families argue and disagree about lots of things, but they are very close. In fact, we will often feel *distant* from each other, even *furious* with one another on the *path* to closeness. That is okay. It is the *effort* we make to be close that God is looking for – in all the different painful and impossible situations in which families find themselves today. (Some people, of course, are in situations where there is just too much pain and abuse and *dis*unity:

if there is serious abuse, professional help or separation may be the only answer.)

So that is the first sign of a church, the first thing that God wants for us. Oneness. Closeness. The trouble is that making time for our families can seem boring – we would rather watch television or stay on at work or clean the house or get lost in some interest. So it is not easy: we will not get there on our own efforts alone. We need to pray for the strength and support of the Spirit, and open our hearts to that.

2. What do you mean by 'holy'?

The second sign or mark of a church is that it is *holy*. Sadly, the word 'holy' has been misunderstood a lot. For hundreds of years, what priests and monks offered families was not very suitable for them. Because they had regular periods of prayer during the day they thought families should have the same – which did not take into account the demands of daily family living. It is a great idea to start the day by kneeling at your bedside to offer your day to God, but **it has been a mistake to think of holiness as being all about prayers and religious practices**.

To be holy is simply to be like God. And God is Love. So holiness for a family is basically about loving. We know that the priest makes Christ more present during the Eucharist, but what we find hard to grasp is that *we* make Christ more present every time we love one another. Jesus is not just found in 'holy' places. He is present when you cook a meal for your family, when you do a kindness for your wife or husband, when you smile at a neighbour, when you are patient with a teenage daughter's tantrum and then make time later to talk with her about her behaviour."

Holiness, then, is about ordinary, earthy things like sex, giving birth, breastfeeding, making dinners, laughing together, shedding tears, giving hugs, wiping snotty noses... They are holy things when they are loving things. In the gospels Jesus points to the importance of the ordinary things like sharing your coat, giving a glass of water, or taking a basin to wash someone. That does not exclude prayer, of course, but it definitely includes the messiness of daily life in a family. Holy is the parent who has scarcely time to pray but who rises at half three in the morning to attend to a child. Holy is the father who comes home from work to enjoy his children, or to teach his daughter to ride a bike, or to challenge his son's neglect of a pet. Holy is the woman who refuses to be a doormat and expects the rest of the family to play their part in cooking and household chores. We do not hear enough that this is holiness – that it is holy to teach children to mend bicycle punctures, it is holy to sit and listen to your wife, it is holy to involve children in doing chores, it is holy to have a picnic or a barbecue with them. When you soothe or hug a child, your arms and your hands are holy, for God is present then. And it is certainly holy to smile and be more positive towards our families, for God is in that smile too. Perhaps the holiest thing of all is to forgive. Lack of forgiveness can destroy family holiness, whereas God leaps into a family where there is forgiveness.

---

*I didn't like my work taking me away from my son, so I told him that Saturday mornings would be just for him from then on, and that I would do whatever **he** wanted me to do on those mornings. So what did he want me to do first? Cycle seven miles to the seaside and have a picnic there! Now, this was December, and I hadn't been on a bike for years! But I got the bikes fixed up during the week, and we headed off on a cold, drizzly morning, and we ate our sandwiches in the rain. And you know something? That's fifteen years ago, and he has left home now, but he told me recently that that is one of his best childhood memories! I had no idea then that what I was doing was 'holy.'*

Holiness, then, is in the ordinary little details of daily living and loving. It includes disappointments, illnesses, hassle, failures, uncooperative children, hostility, being stretched out of our minds... There will be good times, but each family also comes up against hard times and suffering. At those times, when we feel exhausted and shattered and powerless, we can feel anything but holy, yet we may actually be very close to Jesus. For he constantly had to cope with failure, with the bickering of his own little 'family' of disciples, even with their denial and betrayal of him. Holiness is living through all that with love, and with faith and trust in God.

Perhaps you can see now how gentlelove, firmlove and selflove are at the very core of holiness?

3. For every kind of family

Those are two signs. Closeness and holiness. The third sign of a church is catholic (or universal). It simply means 'for all,' 'for everybody.' And for every kind of family.

Some people think, "Holiness isn't for us – it's just for specially good families." That idea certainly does not come from Jesus. It is the most unlikely families that come first for him. Traveller families, disabled families, lone parent families, cohabiting couples, poor families, fighting families, families wracked with drugs and alcohol. They are not only *included* in Christ's church: they are *especially* welcome. Two thousand years ago, the respectable people were very upset that Jesus showed special love for prostitutes, sinners and the poorest and most helpless people. The more needy you are as a family and the greater the sense of failure you may feel, the more you are welcome and loved and invited to be a little church. Who can say that a little broken church is not more special in the eyes of the God of Surprises than one that appears to be healthy?

Catholic means 'for all,' so it needs to be inclusive, meeting people wherever they are at, knowing that **what helps build faith or closeness in one family may not help in another family**. For example, family prayer may work well in one home, and the very mention of it may cause World War Three in another home. One family may sit down and talk things out after a row, but another family may shout and scream – and then get back to normal when one person clears their throat in a particular way. That is okay too. It is the same with meals. Quite a few families never have dinner around a table. Some of them do not even *have* a table, and asking them to eat at a table not only does not work: it makes them feel bad and disheartened. Their time to talk over food may be over a bite of supper in the living room – or over take-away food and a few beers. Being catholic asks us to be open to the different ways God leads us, and to see that there are as many different kinds of family holiness as there are families. So a lone-parent family needs to know that they are just as capable of being holy as a two-parent family. Because God's church is catholic, for everybody, especially for those who *know* they are needy.

4. Reaching out
The fourth sign of a Christian family, of a little church, is not a word we would use every day: apostolic. It means that we are invited to be apostles, like the first apostles. This means many things (including a respect for the tradition and scriptures of the Church), but it invites us, above all, not to keep Christ's love to ourselves, to bring it out to the world around us.

Reaching out to others in love is not just something 'nice' to do. It is the dynamo that drives the little church of the home. When Jesus prayed 'that they may be one,' it was so that we would make a difference to others, for he added, 'so that the *world* may believe it was you who sent me.' If we are just a close family and do not look out to the community around us, we may be missing that point. It is good to ask how our community is different because of our family.

It is not only a matter of spending more time with the family. Reaching out to the poor is as essential to our identity as a Christian family as worship is.
James and Kathy McGinnis, in **Parenting for Peace and Justice**

For most of us being 'apostolic' does not mean going off to the foreign missions. It is about things we do in our own neighbourhood. Sometimes it means big things like fostering a child. Or it might be something like joining Samaritans or the Vincent de Paul Society, or training a junior football team. For some periods in a family's life, it may be impossible to do *much* outside the home, but we can always be apostolic in praying for people – even in *smiling* at them! – in visiting someone who is lonely, or in having a welcoming open house. We all know homes where the children of the neighbourhood are welcome – such a family makes a difference to the community they live in! Many families are *already* little apostolic churches without even realising it. *You* may not be able to do much, but the widow's mite that you give of your time or money or energy does make God more present in your family and in the world.

What might ordinary families do to become more apostolic? You know your own limits, but here are a few areas to consider.

- Go out of your way to invite people in need to eat with you, perhaps on Sundays – an estranged cousin, an elderly aunt, a nephew with a young family...
- Help with the local swimming club or football team.
- Visit someone who is ill.
- Look out for an elderly neighbour – or a young family.
- Adopt a Charity as a family (with sponsored walks, etc.)
- Involve your family in recycling waste.
- Give a percentage of wages, pocket money, etc., to the poor (if everyone in the West gave one percent of their earnings to the poor, that would be enough to end world poverty!)

See if you can also *involve* your children in caring for the needs of others. If you are involved in the community yourself, it will usually be easier to involve a child: 'Speak with your hands before you open your mouth' was a favourite saying of St Peter Claver. You might talk to your children about any community work you are involved in, and ask them to pray for the people you meet there.

Different shapes in different families
So those are the four marks or signs of the church. That is what the Holy Spirit wants for your family. Each of them is flexible: they

take different shapes in different families. In one family, being loving may mean doing *more* things for each other; in another family it may mean doing *fewer* things if you have been doing too much for your children all along. Similarly, some families go camping and get up early to be filled with wonder at God's glory in the dawn – while the rest of us are sleeping sound and could think of nothing worse than to be out in a field so early! Some families are great at hospitality. Some families are wonderful at making music together. Others do great things to support Amnesty International's work for peace and justice; others care about the uneven distribution of wealth in the world. So it is okay and normal and good that each family emphasises different things and finds its own way to be holy.

Summing up
In this chapter we have looked at what the Holy Spirit wants for a family – to make it a little church. This idea is not new, but it is only now beginning to filter down to families from the Second Vatican Council. It can sound like so much jargon until we tease out the meaning of the word 'church.' Then we are more likely to be inspired and to see that holiness in the home is about the ordinary things, about being a warm, responsible, listening parent, that it includes disciplining children, having fun together, talking out tensions, caring about others and making a difference in our communities.

We are not suggesting that religious practices do not have a place. What we are saying is that loving one another in the midst of the daily hassle and messy details of family living is at the *core* of holiness. St John tells us that **this is the great mark or sign of the church: notice the love they have for one another**. Too often in the past, parents were told to *pray* more with their children and it was overlooked that they needed to *play* more with them.

Prayer and religious practices *also* have their place, however, and that is what we will be looking at in the next chapter.

GETTING IN TOUCH

Below are some things that can be spiritual for a family. Tick any that you think might be spiritual or holy for you or your family:

Teaching children to ride bikes.
Being warm, gentle, good-humoured.
Letting children live (within reason) with the consequences of what they do.
Taking 10-15 minutes daily 'space' to catch up as a couple.
Settling your child to bed with a chat, prayers and a blessing.
Having a relaxed late breakfast on Saturday/Sunday mornings.
Being involved in a choir or band, training a team, or working for those in need.
Keeping connected with parents, family, relatives.
Having a picnic or a barbecue.
Attending church together.
Going through a photo album together – or making one!
Making love with your spouse, or being physically close.
Having bedtime chats/ stories.
Hugging, touch, play-wrestling.
Being part of a local support group of families.
Playing cards, board games, outdoor games, with the family.
Supporting charities/ missions.
Being real with your children about what you think and feel and what's important to you.
Praying as a couple.

Planning trips together – cycling, the cinema, a nature walk...
Attending a parenting or marriage course.
Praying before meals.
Being available to listen, talk, do homework, play...
Slowing down to do things *along* with a child, not just on your own – gardening, cooking, washing dog...
Celebrating birthdays/occasions.
Watching TV or a video together.
Welcoming neighbours/ local children at your home.
Treats – ice cream, chocolate, flowers, doing someone's chore...
Remembering to ask about the *details* of your child's life.
Being committed to recycling.
Taking space and doing things *you* enjoy – for your family's sake.
Regularly praying *for* your family and for those in need.
Having a weekly 'date' with your partner – a film, walk, good chat...
Befriending an elderly couple – and maybe having them baby-sit for you.
Hanging loose around the kitchen or living room where the 'craic' is.
Shopping, gardening, laundry...
Talking out tensions and forgiving/ making up after a row.
Having a regular weekly time to plan some of the things above.

CASE STUDY

It's nine o'clock in the evening. Dad, as a result of attending a programme for his daughter Daniela's Confirmation, has decided that he wants to be more available to his two children, spending some fun-time with them. He asks them if they would like to play a game of cards, and he is open to whatever game *they* would like to play, even if it means that they have to teach him how to play it. He also realises that *enjoying* the children is more important than winning, so he has decided that he is not interested in winning the game. The children are pleased with the suggestion and the game starts. While they are playing, however, a neighbour, Joe Byrne, drops in. Dad makes him welcome and invites him to join them.

"Oh, no, no," Joe protests. "I've called at a bad time. I'll come back another time."

Everyone insists, however, that Joe should stay and play with them, so he sits down at the table and joins in the game.

Questions for discussion:
Can you see ways in which this family was a little church – with any of the four marks of the church:
1. How were they answering Jesus' prayer 'that they may be one...'?
2. How was what they were doing holy – bearing in mind that God is love and anything that is loving is holy?
3. And how were they being catholic and apostolic, i.e., including everyone, being a sign to others, reaching out to others...

LOOKING AHEAD: MAKING PLANS

Underline two things on the previous page that you will do with your family this week. (You may like to come back to this page each weekend and use it to help you plan for your family.)

My Plans:

_____

_____

- Take 15 minutes in the next few days to read chapter 2. If your course has just two sessions, it may be important to plan how and when you will read the rest of the book in stages.

Chapter 3: How can we pray when we have a million things to do?

*"Don't talk to me about religious practices in the home. We're miles away from all that. I'm not saying I'm happy about it. My faith means a lot to me and I'm sad to see the children drifting today. But life is just so hectic and pressured now. And... it's more than that – I was bored as a child by the Rosary and all the prayers that were just rhymed off, and there's no way my children would put up with that boredom today. I just don't know what to put in its place – for them **or** for myself!"*

This cry from the heart of a parent echoes what is happening for many families today. Some parents no longer use traditional prayers (though there is certainly value in them, and they still mean a lot to many parents). These parents do not feel good about the lack of family prayer, but they feel inadequate and do not know where to start. As one mother said, "Pass on the faith? I can't even get the children to pass the salt!" Hopefully, then, you will find some practical suggestions in this chapter to make things easier.

A bird prays!
A first step is to broaden our idea of what prayer is. Are you
aware that a tree prays? That a bird prays? That a flower prays?
For they certainly do. They give glory to God just by being the
tree or the bird or the flower that God created them to be. In the
same way, *we* pray and give glory to God just by being loving
persons – as God created us to be. In other words, **to love is to
pray. Daily living and loving that is in harmony with God is
prayer: how we work, how we spend our spare time, how we
speak to others – and about others – how we live our lives for
twenty-four hours a day. That is our real prayer.** It is much
more than the prayer of a tree or a plant, of course, because
(through Baptism, Confirmation and the Eucharist) we are part of
the Body of Christ on earth and the Holy Spirit prays within us.

Our prayer, then, is how we live. Thomas Merton says we pray
by the way we walk or talk or even pick things up. Isn't that what
Scripture means when we are asked to 'pray always'? Here is a
story that may help to illustrate that.

"No peace to pray!"
A father told us recently about a special moment in his life. He is
someone who goes off to a corner of the house to pray for a
quarter of an hour every evening, and on this occasion he was
praying for openness to whatever God wanted. His wife came in
and told him she had a cramp across her shoulders. "Sit down," he
said, rising from his chair, "and I'll try massaging your shoulders."
Five minutes or so later, the pain had eased and she left. He
settled back to pray, but his eight-year-old daughter burst in.

"Dad, come quick," she said, "There's a daddy-long-legs in the
bedroom and I'm scared of it." Dealing with it took quite a while
because he wanted to free it through the window. Eventually he
got back to pray to find that his prayer time had run out. But here
is the point of the story.

"A year ago," this man said, "I would have felt angry and
frustrated that I wasn't getting any peace to pray. But here I was
getting a clear message that I was praying when I was massaging

my wife's shoulders and I was praying when I was dealing with my daughter's fears. God is teaching me," he said, "that meeting interruptions with love during prayer-time is an even better prayer. In fact, I'm learning that acting with love at *any* time is a prayer because Christ is present whenever there is love."

To love is to pray
The point he made seems to be a vital one, that prayer is not just 'saying prayers,' that to love is to pray. Being open to *anything* that helps us to be led by love is a prayer. Thinking about someone with compassion. Listening well during Mass. Doing a parenting course. Having a chat with another parent about our children. Even spending a weekend away as a couple that allows us to come back with more energy for our children and for each other. And it is most certainly a prayer to sit down before bedtime and say to myself, "I've planned what I'll do for work tomorrow. Now, how can I plan some good family time? Mm... I'll get Joe to help me bake an apple-tart... And I'll get him to show me his new game..."

There is always a temptation to put religious practices and 'saying prayers' into a little pigeonhole separate from the living and loving of our daily lives. But St John tells us (1 John 4) that **it is pointless to say, "I love you," to God unless I am making an effort to love those around me.** We have already seen that lots of praying time was important to the monks who shaped our ideas of holiness, and they did not seem to realise that *family* holiness is quite different – that to change nappies is to pray, to laugh with your family is to pray, to forgive hurtful words is to pray, to train children to cook is to pray...

Without realising it, then, you may be praying a lot more than you think, and one of the goals of this book is to make you aware of that. When Jesus summed up his life's work at the Last Supper, he did not mention loving God: he said, "Love one another just as I have loved you." He did not need to talk about God because he knew that God is always there flowing through us as soon as we give ourselves in love to others. On the last day you may be

31

among those astonished people who say, "But we hardly had time
to pray! When did we do all these things?" And Jesus will reply,
"When you showed love to the least of these, you did it to me."

---

*The Church teaches that family prayer is not just 'saying prayers'
but that it involves: "joys and sorrows, hopes and
disappointments, birth and birthday celebrations, wedding
anniversaries of the parents, departures, separations and
homecomings, important and far-reaching decisions, the death of
those that are near, etc. all of these mark God's loving
intervention in the family's history."*
Pope John Paul II, in *Familiaris Consortio*, 59

Times of awareness
To love is to pray, then. But most of us need something to *remind*
us to be patient and loving in what we do. **One great help is to
turn our minds to God at passing moments of the day.** As I go
for a walk, I can be in touch with nature and simply be thankful to
God in my heart. When I am feeling frazzled, a powerful prayer
might be, "Help me get through this day!" – or "I'm sorry, God,
for losing my patience just now. Help me to make up to him." Or
sometimes we find ourselves worrying about a child and we forget
to turn that worry into a prayer, "Dear God, I'm worried about
Martin. Please look after him. I trust in you." When we tune in to
God like that, it becomes easier to *act* lovingly.

Recently, for example, a mother was settling her son to bed.
She had chatted with him and put out the light when he said,
"Mum, I'm thirsty." Now, she knew he was probably just playing
for time, but she explained, "Something clicked with me at that
moment, 'If you give a drink of water in my name...'" And she
went and got him the water. To become aware like this can be a
little 'God-moment' that gives us the energy to love and can help
us to live our lives more in harmony with God.

What might help us remember to turn to God like this so that we have more love in our lives? Some people find it helps to begin a task at home (gardening, cooking, cleaning, even relaxing with a cuppa!) by making the sign of the cross. Others are reminded to pray when their watch pips on the hour. Others use a pen and notebook to get in touch with what is going on in their lives at present, and they find that this is a way of leading them into the presence of God. It can be helpful, too, to pray before making a decision about the children or before having a serious talk with someone in the family.

There are also some situations where prayer arises naturally. When someone sneezes, people often say, "God bless you!" At the end of a phone call or a visit, we often say, "God bless!" or "Take care!" These can be empty words – but they *can* be a prayer for that person when we are aware of what we are saying.

What we say can also show our faith to our children. For example, when a child is upset we might listen and understand, but we can then remind the child, "Remember too that God is taking care of you." So God is not separated from their daily lives. In the same way, if you pray silently at the start of a journey, that may help *you* to be aware of God, but if you can feel free to pray *aloud*, then *others* become aware – and can learn from your faith.

Your faith is the key!
Maybe you expected this chapter to focus on prayer and religious practices with children. We will move on to look at that now, but I hope you can see that your *own* love and faith are the keys to building faith in the home. Children are more likely to value prayer when they see that *you* value prayer. **They will probably learn more about Mass, for example, from the expression on your face *during* Mass than from any other source.**

You may find that difficult to believe if your children are already reacting against Mass and prayer – "this is so weird!" Parents of older children often feel discouraged when their children give up all practice of their faith and no longer attend church. You may think then that there is no faith left in your home. If *you*, however, keep love in your heart and have faith and trust in God, then there is most certainly faith in your home – even when you feel everything else is falling apart! Good parents have worried about their children's faith for many centuries, but we need to trust and hand them over to a loving God whose ways are not our ways!

Now, what about the details of praying with children?

Allow for differences
The hardest thing about writing this section is that each family is so different. In some families, spoken prayer comes naturally, but in most families it does not. In many families there are no times at all when they pray together – and huge resistance to any change! So we would like to look at some possibilities without adding to any guilt that some of you may feel.

Even if a family does have regular prayer times, **it is easy to forget that prayer needs to keep changing. There are obviously big differences, for example, between the prayer of a seven-year-old and that of a fourteen-year-old. What was suitable last year will probably not suit this year.** For one thing, your child may be less open to praying *with* you. Last year, you could join your son at bedtime and prayer came easily. Now he is not so sure about you invading his space. One way of respecting his privacy is to have more periods of silence. "We'll take a minute to pray in silence for our own needs and the needs of others." Or, "Let's think about how we loved and didn't love today, and talk to God in our hearts about that."

Ideas for praying with children
Having a time of silence like this is one way of praying with your child. If you prefer to use prayers that have been learnt by heart, you might say them more slowly now that your children are older, pausing to allow time to let the prayer sink in. For example, in saying the Act of Sorrow at bedtime, *"I'll pause during this prayer to let the meaning of it sink in: O my God, we thank you for loving us... (pause) We're sorry for all our sins... (pause) For not loving*

others and not loving you... (pause) *Help us to live like Jesus...*
(pause) *And not to sin again..."* (pause) In Appendix 1 you will
find a collection of common prayers, including the mysteries of the
rosary. (If a full rosary seems too long, you might like to say a
single decade of it with your child.)

As they enter on a new stage in their lives, your children may
also be more ready to pray from the heart – though they may not
want to tell you what they are praying about! Or they may be
ready to start praying with scripture. (In Appendix 2 of this book,
there are a number of simple ways of using a scripture story for
prayer with children.) Some parents also like to bless their
children at bedtime. Many of us have grown up thinking that only
priests can bless, but *anyone* can put their hands on another
person's head or shoulder and pray, *"God bless you and keep you
safe during the night."* Or you can speak that blessing as you trace
the sign of the cross on their forehead with holy water. And
perhaps you could also ask your child to bless *you?*

When you join your child for a chat and prayer at bedtime, by
the way, it is good to think of the chat as *part* of the prayer,
whether you are talking about football or pop music or whatever.
But it is a good idea also to have a chat sometimes about what you
believe. You could *stretch* their faith a little, for example, when
you let them know that **when they wash dishes it is a prayer,
that when they vacuum the floor, eat together, do their
homework, play games, etc., those are all things that (to use a
human term) bring a smile to God's eyes.**

Mealtimes

Many families pray before meals. It is a good habit to build – it
can slow you down and help you to remember that meals are not
just eat-and-run times. "Thank you for this food, God. Help us to
slow down and catch up on one another during the meal. And
please bless all the people in the hospital who are looking after
granny and the other patients." (That is a 'little church' prayer,
because it is really asking that we be one and holy as we chat over

the food, and it is also catholic and apostolic in thinking of the needs of people beyond the home.)

I had been snappy and moody with everyone, and a cloud of depression hung over the table when we sat down to eat. It felt all wrong. So I said, "Look, everyone, I need to apologise. I've been in a rotten mood today and I think I've taken it out on all of you. I'm sorry. Please forgive me." There was no mention of God in what I said, but I think it was a perfect Grace Before Meals for God was at that table in the complete change of mood after that.

It is good to vary your grace before meals, not just always saying something you know by heart. You might ask, "What are some things you'd like to thank God for before we start to eat?" You can bring the needs of others before God, including people in the news and in crisis spots of the world – or you might mention (or encourage your children to mention) people who are in need of prayer. Lighting one or two candles often helps, and this is much more powerful when the lighting becomes part of your grace. For example, *"We'll light the first candle for the past – to remember all our family and friends who have died...* (pause) *And the second candle for the future – to put our lives and our trust in your hands, God.* (pause) *Amen."*

Religious objects?
It has to be said that candles (or pictures, statues, holy water fonts, etc.) do not make a Christian home, but their absence does say something. A crucifix on the wall, or a picture of Jesus or Mary makes a statement about who you are. If you do not like some of the 'sugary' pictures you see for sale there are also many good ones – or you might consider cutting out and framing attractive ones that you find in a book. Some people attach a prayer or a picture to the fridge with a magnet.

A religious object takes on new meaning, however, when you notice or *use* it. Turning towards a crucifix as you pray. Lighting a candle as you say grace. Using the font to bless the children with holy water before they go to sleep – or to bless *yourself* as you leave the house or return home! Children pick up pretty quickly whether something is an object of faith or a mere ornament. There are even some families who have a special 'sacred space' in the home where they gather and light a candle for evening prayer. There may be a picture of Mary there during May (possibly a framed Christmas card), a picture of Jesus during June, the month of the Sacred Heart, a cactus (a reminder of the desert) during Lent, and a crib during Advent and Christmas time.

I was fed up listening to moaning, so during Lent I said, "For Lent this year I would like each of us during the evening meal to say one bad thing that happened that day and two good things." I went first for a few evenings. You can't imagine how much better mealtime was as a result of that one small change. It allowed everyone to tell their stories and have their say.

Using the Church's year
The church calendar offers us lots of opportunities to have family rituals, and they can be **powerful ways to link prayer in the home with what is happening in the wider church.** At Lent, many families make sacrifices and have a soup meal once a week in order to raise money for a 'Third World' Charity. An Advent Calendar helps to build up a sense of waiting and expecting (but not the calendars with a chocolate in each window – they have the opposite effect!) At Easter, a chocolate egg can be broken open on the table with a little ceremony, "Just as an egg breaks open to let new life out, we break this egg as a sign of our new life in Christ – and we're now going to celebrate that by eating the chocolate!" The children will be much more aware of the chocolate than of God, but they will be happy with the jumble of Easter egg and God

being all linked together in their celebration. Faith can be planted and nourished in that way.

Family rituals are not just for obviously 'religious' events, of course. Blowing out the candles before sharing a birthday cake with everyone, joining in the ducking for apples at Halloween, having a regular supper-time, or taking a weekly walk together in the park are little rituals that may make no reference to God, but they are certainly holy. Saying a prayer can help to draw our attention to this holiness. If you go out to a restaurant as a couple to celebrate your anniversary with a meal, for example, you might say a short prayer before you eat, "Thank you, God, for blessing our marriage through the good times and bad times over the past fifteen years." (Note that family prayer is not just for the children!) You might also consider preparing a special meal with a lit candle and a prayer to celebrate an achievement, an exam passed, Mothers' Day, a Church Holy Day –or even the end of a school term (see Appendix 1 for ideas on how you could do this).

On the first Sunday of Advent, instead of having an 'instant' crib, we put the empty crib on a low table. We add the straw on the second Sunday, the animals and manger on the third Sunday, next Mary and Joseph on the fourth Sunday, and finally the baby and the shepherds on Christmas Eve night. Each time we pray, "As we prepare with Mary for Christmas, help us to open our hearts to your love, God, so that we may welcome Christ in everyone we meet. Amen."

Summing up
The main idea of this chapter is that you are already praying more in your daily life than you may have thought – because to love is to pray. When you pray, "Come, Holy Spirit" the Spirit answers, *"Certainly. Just keep on loving. Your love opens the path for me to flow through you and your family."*   It can be a great relief to

understand this instead of feeling guilty if you find it impossible to have formal family prayer.

We saw that it is easier to keep on loving when I am *aware* of God in snatches of prayer through the day. In other words, family prayer begins with a parent's own love and faith. We moved on then to look at prayer with children. There is no suggestion that families should neglect traditional prayers or practices which they find helpful, but they do need to have the freedom to look at other approaches and find what works best for them in their different situations.

If the chapter has made you aware of new possibilities for your family, that is great, but you will never get it all together – and this is a difficult area for many families. In most homes, family prayer (when it does happen) is interrupted and messy and will often feel a bit ragged. But if you are finding things tough, if life (and your family) makes you humble and aware of how little you can do without trusting in a power much greater than your own, be happy, because that humility is the great shortcut to God.

CASE STUDY

Mary Butler joined her son Gary at bedtime. She usually found this the best time of the day for catching up on his life, for that was when he talked to her about friends and teachers, sport, television, music and so on. After the chat, she said, "I'll have to go now, so we'll just take a moment in silence to thank God for all the blessings of today." After a little silence, she said, "And we'll say sorry in our hearts for any times you can think of when we *failed* to love today..." Then she kissed him good night.

*This is just one form of prayer. There is no suggestion that this is the 'right' way. What do you like and dislike about it? Do you see the chat and the kiss as **part** of their prayer?*

LOOKING AHEAD: MAKING PLANS

1. It starts with you. How could you become more aware of God in your daily life, perhaps with occasional short prayers? What might be good times? When you get out of bed in the morning? As you prepare food? Before you eat? As you travel to work? As you start work? As you prepare to meet your children after work? Prayer with a child will come more naturally when *you* pray during the day.

2. With your child. What will you do this week to pray with at least one member of your family? If you have done little praying with children to date, it may be wise to move *gradually* in introducing prayer at home. You might start with a chat at bedtime. A week or so later, you might introduce the short 'Night Prayer' from Appendix 1 at the end of your chat. When your child is used to that, it may be time to begin saying a short grace before meals. If you already do these things, you might look at the sections on prayer at the back of this book, see what you think might be helpful, and plan to use something there.

Some plans for the future: _____

_____

- Please read chapter 3 in the next week – and take a look at the ideas on praying with children in Appendix 1. Closer to the Confirmation Day you may find it useful to read chapter 4 (about the sacrament of Confirmation and how it fits into your family life). It is also a great idea to take ten minutes now and again to look back over a section of this book. You will get much more out of it if you take time to do that – and to use the prayer sections at the back.

Chapter 4: Questions about Confirmation

"I wonder how much money will I get for Confirmation?" That is
the biggest question about Confirmation in the minds of many
young girls and boys. And that is okay. Like the presents at
Christmas, receiving Confirmation money can be all part of the
excitement and celebration of a special occasion.

In the minds of parents other questions loom. *"Where will I get
the money for new clothes?"* *"Will we have a meal at home, or
will we go out?"* These questions are important too – there is
something wonderful about the generosity of parents who want to
spend their last penny on clothes and on a meal to make their child
special and to celebrate with grandparents or other relatives. God
loves to see us celebrating!

But this book is also written to help you see how Confirmation
fits into the wider picture of what you most want for your family.
In this chapter, we'd like to link together all the various ideas of
the course as well as dealing with some of the common questions
parents ask about Confirmation.

Where does it come from?
We'll begin by looking at where the sacrament of Confirmation
comes from. It all began on Pentecost Sunday. With the power of

a whirlwind the Holy Spirit swept through the friends of Jesus who had gathered together in the room, sweeping aside their fears and all the things that usually block people from changing. The result was almost unbelievable. People who had been full of fear were filled with the spirit of love for others. They stopped worrying about money and security – from then on they shared what they had with others who were not so well off. People who had been running scared, worrying about what everybody else thought of them, had become a church. The church was born. That's what happens when the Holy Spirit, the love between God the Lover and God the Beloved, catches fire inside us. We don't know how many languages the apostles could speak. What we do know is that the chief language they spoke was the language of love. Everybody understands it. People who have love in their hearts don't need words. "By this will everyone know that you are my disciples, if you have love one for another."

That is the kind of loving community a family is invited to be. And that is what happens when we allow the Holy Spirit to blow through us and make us channels of God's love in our families. The little church of the home is given new life again.

Why does the Holy Spirit not have the same dramatic effect on us as on the apostles in the upper room?
There is one major difference. Preparation. The apostles had spent weeks praying earnestly for the Spirit. *And* they had spent three years close to a person who was filled and led by the Holy Spirit, Jesus himself. That was some preparation for the sacrament! But it is also a challenge to us. The best preparation a child can have is to be with people (especially parents) who allow themselves, like Jesus, to be filled with and led by the Spirit.

The best preparation a child can have is to be with people (especially parents) who, like Jesus, allow themselves to be filled with and led by the Spirit.

That is not as far-fetched as it may sound. After all, we parents have also been confirmed. The Spirit is knocking at the door of our hearts, whispering, *"Remember that you are mine. Let me bring alive the sacrament of Confirmation in you. Open yourself to me and let's both co-operate in setting fire to these lovely children of ours on their Confirmation day and throughout their entire lives."*

"Remember that you are mine. Let me bring alive the sacrament of Confirmation in you. Open yourself to me and let's both co-operate in setting fire to these lovely children of ours on their Confirmation day and throughout their entire lives."

What does that mean – to co-operate with the Spirit?
That is what we have been looking at right through this book. Co-operating with the Holy Spirit means taking seriously the invitation to love one another and letting ourselves be led more and more by love.

Can you imagine living like that for even one day at a time? You smile at shop assistants and say thanks to them. If you have a car, you let waiting cars out of side roads (within reason) instead of just driving from A to B. You say less to your family – you listen instead and ask about their concerns and the details of their lives. You go the extra mile in your thoughtfulness to others. You surprise someone in your family with a hug, a chocolate bar, or suggesting a game with them. In other words, you let them know that they are more important to you than your work, that you are available to them.

Those are examples of gentlelove. But you also co-operate with the Spirit by showing firmlove and a proper degree of self-love. You take time out to relax instead of over-working, and you encourage others to be responsible and to play their part in doing chores, etc. Those are all ways of being led by the Spirit of Love and letting your life with your family become a prayer.

For this to happen, we have seen how much it helps to turn our minds to God from time to time during the day. We can make a short prayer as we get out of bed, have a meal, travel, work, relax or whatever. All that helps to open us to the Holy Spirit and bring alive our own sacrament of Confirmation.

We have also seen that another way to co-operate with the Spirit is to have a regular weekly time for planning. That might include: 1. Planning to take care of yourself as a person (including planning to build up the habit of praying at key moments through the day). 2. Planning time for yourselves as a couple (or with your friends/wider family, if you are not a couple). 3. Planning to set aside time to make good connections with your children (on page 27 there are lots of good ideas for doing this). If you like this idea of planning, it may be good to ask yourself if there is a fixed time at weekends that might suit for it.

We have seen how it helps to turn our minds to God from time to time during the day. We can make a short prayer as we get out of bed, have a meal, travel, work, relax or whatever. All that helps to open us to the Holy Spirit and bring alive our own sacrament of Confirmation.

What actually happens at the ceremony of Confirmation?
The Bishop stretches out his hands over the group to be confirmed, praying to God, "Send your Holy Spirit upon them to be their helper and guide…" Then he rests his hand on the head of each person being confirmed and makes the sign of the cross on the forehead with his thumb. At the same time, the sponsor stands behind the young person with a hand on the right shoulder. After this anointing with oil, the bishop gives the sign of peace, saying, "Peace be with you," and the young person replies, "And also with you."

A LITTLE BIT OF HISTORY

In the early days of the Church, most people becoming Christians were adults, not children, and were called catechumens. Before Baptism they spent quite some time being instructed, being taught to pray and being helped to become more loving.

When they were ready, they were led down three steps (reminding them of the three days in the tomb) into the waters of a big baptismal font, often shaped like a tomb. Next – and they weren't always expecting this – their heads were ducked under the water and held there for a while. They came up spluttering and gasping for breath. (Later they were asked what that felt like, and they would say something like, "I thought I was dying!" "Exactly," the sponsor would say, "You've got it – you die with Christ in Baptism and then rise again – you'll remember that for a long time!") After being ducked three times, in the name of the Father, the Son and the Holy Spirit, the baptised person was led up out of the 'tomb' and confirmed straight away, rubbed with sweet-smelling oil just as athletes were in those days to be strengthened for a race. A white robe was then put on (as we still do with a baby at baptism) as a sign of their new life in Christ. Finally, as if two sacraments in one day were not enough, they were led from the vestry straight into the church where an enthusiastic crowd of other Christians greeted them warmly, and they went up during that Mass to make their First Communion. So they received three sacraments on the same day, Baptism, Confirmation and Eucharist. Note the order, by the way, because some people think that children today should receive the sacrament of Confirmation *before* they receive Communion, as they did in the early Church.

Those three sacraments together make us full members of the Body of Christ. To bring out the close connection between them, you will notice on your child's Confirmation Day that the Confirmation takes place *during* a Mass and includes the reception of Holy Communion – and a renewal of the promises made at Baptism. That is closer to how Confirmation was celebrated in the early Church.

I'm not sure what you mean by the word 'anointing'?
To anoint simply means to rub oil on someone. Kings, prophets and priests have always been anointed to do the tasks God gave them. At Confirmation we are anointed with chrism (a mixture of olive oil and a perfumed ointment called balsam), to share in Christ's work as priest (worshipping God), prophet (witnessing to others by our example) and king (leading others by serving them in love). The very word Christ *means* 'the anointed one.'

How does the sponsor fit in?
During the Confirmation ceremony, the sponsor stands behind the young person with a hand on their right shoulder, as if to say, "The rest of us are behind you, supporting you, giving you example and encouragement."

It may be important, then, to think before choosing a sponsor. It cannot be the child's parent, as the sponsor's task is to *support* the parents. Ideally it will be the godparent (since Confirmation is so closely linked with Baptism), but if he or she is not suitable, someone with good values and strong faith might be chosen. In the early Church, a sponsor gave a lot of support, before and afterwards, to the person being confirmed, and it would be great once more to see sponsors playing a more vital part in a young person's life.

Do people have to take a new name at Confirmation?
It is not essential: it just depends on what is done in your area. In some places, the Baptism name only is used – to emphasise the close link between Confirmation and Baptism. In other places a new name is taken, just as Abram's name was changed to Abraham and Saul's to Paul after an important spiritual event in their lives.

You might consider borrowing a book of saints' lives from the library and talking to your child about choosing the name of a saint who attracts them and can be a special patron saint for them for the rest of their lives. When they have decided on a name, see if you can find a book about the saint they have chosen – the life of a saint can be inspiring to a young person, and reading it can be an excellent preparation for Confirmation. Or you might encourage your child to think about choosing the name of a grandparent who has died and who is now a saint with a special interest in that child!

See if you can find a book about the saint they have chosen – the life of a saint can be inspiring to a young person, and reading it may be an excellent preparation for Confirmation

---

What does the bishop say to the person being confirmed?
He addresses the person, using the new name, "(Name), be sealed with the gift of the Holy Spirit," and the young person replies, "Thanks be to God." The Spirit is called a gift because a gift is freely given, not earned. And it is given especially to those who *ask* for it. In fact, prayer is highlighted in almost every instance of the receiving of the Holy Spirit in the New Testament. It is good, then, to build up a stronger desire in ourselves and in our children for the gift of the Spirit. A simple prayer like "Come, Holy Spirit, open our hearts to love others" is quite suitable – or even just "Come!" Those who ask always receive the gift of the Spirit.

Aren't there lots of gifts of the Spirit?
Well, the real gift *is* the Spirit of God in our hearts, but the special gifts of that Spirit are wisdom and understanding, right judgement and courage, knowledge and reverence, wonder and awe in God's presence. There are also many, many gifts of the Spirit, as you can see in the powerful things done in Jesus. The Spirit wants to continue to do these powerful things in Jesus' Body, the Church. The Acts of the Apostles tells how the Body of Christ in the early Church did many of the same things as Jesus had done, and in every age there are wonderful examples of how the Spirit moves in the lives of the Saints – and in ordinary families! You know the Spirit is moving in your life when you see the fruits of the Spirit.

What are the fruits of the Spirit?
They are qualities you can see in people who open themselves to
the Holy Spirit. St Paul lists them as love, joy, peace, patience,
kindness, goodness, gentleness, faithfulness and self-control. A
simple way to look at them, however, is to think of them all as
love. It has been said that joy is love dancing, peace is love
resting, patience is love waiting, kindness is love giving and
caring, goodness is love shining through, gentleness is love acting,
faithfulness is love lasting, and self-control is love respecting.
Parents should not worry if they do not see these fruits of the Spirit
in their children immediately: the seeds planted in Baptism and
Confirmation may take a long time before they grow into strong
plants that bear fruit like this. With good care, though, that growth
comes eventually. If *you* open yourself more and more to the Holy
Spirit, you need have no worry about your children. The love in
your heart and the energy of the Spirit will do its slow work of
converting them, though it may take years...

You probably know the story of St Augustine. The lovely,
bright, intelligent child who broke his mother's heart. He had no
time for his parents' religion, he wanted to do his own thing, enjoy
life, live it up. So he lived for years like a pagan. His mother
Monica, like many parents today, was filled with sadness to see
her child throwing his life away. She had a strong sense of failure.
But she didn't despair. For years she kept praying and praying for
her son. And eventually her example and her prayers won
through. Augustine realised that he was not at peace, that nothing
but God's love could satisfy his heart. It was then he spoke his
famous words, "You have made us for yourself, God, and our
hearts are restless until they rest in you." That is a lovely prayer to
teach our children, even if the meaning of it does not register with
them until years later.

---

*If you open yourself more and more to the Holy Spirit, you need
have no worry about your children.*

No matter how bad things seem in your family, then, there is no point in despairing. You are not on your own. As St Monica discovered, the Holy Spirit of Love always wins through in the end.

Is taking a pledge about drugs one of the fruits of the Spirit?
In some dioceses, young people being confirmed are encouraged to make a promise or pledge about drugs – to abstain from alcohol until they are more mature and to abstain from other drugs for life. This works best, however, when the pledge is not an automatic thing but something that is talked out. It is certainly a fruit of the Spirit when a young person knows what is involved and makes a mature decision to resist today's powerful pressures to abuse drugs.

Has there been a change of emphasis in Confirmation?
Yes. The Vatican Council has brought us closer to the spirit of the Early Church. Before the Council, people tended to see Confirmation as the sacrament of independence, helping me personally to be a stronger Christian. Today there is more understanding of the Holy Spirit's work in drawing us *together* in the Body of Christ, drawing us closer to our families and helping us to care for other people, especially those who are in need or on the margins of society. The gift of the Spirit, in other words, is to deepen the love between us as a 'little church' of the home in order to reach out to others beyond the home.

Is there not too much talk about 'love'? What about fasting and self-denial – have they gone out the window?
There is nothing easy about love. It is full of self-denial. Love often means giving up comforts and going against my feelings for the sake of another. It asks me to take up the cross – getting out of bed cheerfully in the morning, being patient with a teenager, settling a child to bed at night... Our controlled little world falls apart when we become parents and are led where we do not want to go. That is what it means to die with Christ!

There is no merit at all in suffering for the sake of suffering. Fasting and self-denial still have their place, but only when they help us to be more loving. Whenever we feel the pain of doing without something, whenever we feel frustrated, misunderstood, depressed, that is a time to turn our suffering into an act of love with a prayer, "I'm feeling depressed and weary, God. Help me so that I don't punish or upset others!" In that way, you are not just fooling yourself with *feelings* of love or pious words, you have your feet on the ground and can really mean what you say.

There is no merit at all in suffering for the sake of suffering! Fasting and self-denial still have their place, but only when they help us to be more loving.

If we pray to the Spirit, are we not neglecting Jesus and the Father?
At different times in your life you may prefer to pray to one of the persons of the Trinity rather than another. That is normal, and not something to worry about. Remember, though, that we are made in the image of the Trinity (persons in love), so the best prayer we can make to God is to *be* that image – persons in love – doing our best to live more loving lives and attempting to give ourselves, like Jesus in the Eucharist, to be shared by others.

We *also* need to get to know Jesus, of course, so that we may love and follow him, but that *is* the work of the Spirit and will certainly draw us to the Father too. In Appendix 2 and in the Resources page at the back of this book you will find suggestions for getting to know Jesus better.

Life's journey
In this book we have put less emphasis on a once-off Confirmation Day. Instead, we have looked at how the Spirit works with parents in the daily confirming of their families' faith. The emphasis is on our whole journey through life rather than on one day.

That journey started with Baptism. When a child is baptised, the ceremony starts at the door to the church, moves to the book of the scriptures, then to the font, and ends at the altar. That 'journey' is to remind us of the journey we all take through life, beginning with entry into the Church and ending as full members of the Body of Christ, fed at the altar of the Eucharist.

For most families this will not be a journey that *feels* very spiritual. It can be hard to believe that the daily grind of working and eating and squabbling is the path to holiness. But that is family spirituality – rooted in all the messy details of ordinary daily life in the home. That is where the Spirit moves. Through our daily loving and faith the Spirit of God gradually changes a family and forms it into a cell of the Body of Christ, a little church whose love overflows into the world around us. In our own small way each family can make a difference. That is the good news announced by Jesus and restated in the teachings of the Second Vatican Council. It can be hard to take it in, because we are so used to plodding through life, often feeling inadequate and unspiritual and very ordinary. We can even feel overwhelmed with guilt, forgetting that we are not alone, that we have a powerful friend in the Holy Spirit whom we received in our own Baptism and Confirmation. Hopefully we now have a better sense of where that friend wants to lead us.

Summary

In this chapter, we looked at what happens in the ceremony of Confirmation and we teased out a little of what it can mean for the person being confirmed and for their family.

Maybe the most important challenge of the chapter is that our children need *us parents* to be people who are open to the Spirit if Confirmation is to be fully effective. We saw that this openness invites us to be holy in our ordinary daily lives – in how we practise gentlelove, firmlove and proper self-love. And we have seen how helpful it is to turn our minds to God at times throughout the day and to ask Jesus for his Spirit of love in dealing with the chores and frustrations of daily living.

It is not easy to be a parent today. At times it may seem as if faith is almost dead in our families, and we may feel a deep sense of failure. At times like that, we can be very close to Jesus whose own life's work seemed to have failed. We can then turn to him in humility and faith and trust, remembering that our *attempt* to keep loving is all he looks for. He will take care of the rest.

When some people were walking away from Jesus, he turned to Peter and asked, "Will you also go away?" Peter's reply was, "Where else can we go?" In other words, there is nothing else in life that makes as much sense. Making money is not the answer. Or giving my life to a job. Or becoming famous. Or living to eat and drink. No matter what the media may say, there is no real alternative to the search for God. We may find satisfaction for a while in other things, but only the Spirit of Jesus can bring us the peace and joy and love for which our hearts have been made.

There is nothing else in life that makes as much sense. Making money is not the answer. Or giving my life to a job. Or becoming famous. Or living to eat and drink. There is no real alternative to the search for God.

APPENDIX 1: PRAYING WITH CHILDREN

PRAYING AT BEDTIME

There are many ways of praying, and there is no need to change your own way as long as it seems to work for you. But as children become more self-conscious and 'private' here is one suggestion that some parents can use or adapt:

You join a child for a chat at bedtime. That is often a good time to talk, for your son or daughter may want to hold on to you a little longer. Enjoy the chat – it is an act of love so it is part of your prayer. After the chat, you might say:

"We'll just take a moment to thank God for all the blessings of today.." (Silence for a short period – but if either of you wish, you can mention something you are thankful for.)

"Let's think for a moment about how we loved and didn't love today, and talk to God in our hearts about that…" (Silence again for a short period – but either of you is free to speak.) **"And we'll say sorry in our hearts for any times we can think of when we** *failed* **to love today…"** (short pause)

"And we'll take a minute to pray in silence for our own needs and the needs of others…" (Again, feel free to speak.)

Finally, you might bless your child, either with a hand on the shoulder or (after dipping a finger in holy water) tracing the sign of the cross on the forehead as you say something like: **"God bless you and keep you safe always."**

The prayer above respects a young person's privacy, but it is good to say some of your prayer aloud at times and thus expose your child to your own faith – you might say what *you* want to thank God for, or mention something you did during the day that you want to say sorry to God for. You can also vary this prayer in your own way. And you might ask your child to bless you.

There is nothing magic about holy water, of course – you could explain that blessing with holy water is a reminder of our life in Christ through Baptism. Indeed, a good Confirmation gift might be an attractive holy water font for your child's bedroom. You will need to remember to keep it topped up and you might encourage your child to use it first thing in the morning and last thing at night.

SET PRAYERS

Many of the prayers on the next pages are prayers that your children have learned at school and may have said a little mechanically up to now, without much thought. Encourage them to say these prayers more slowly now that they are older, so that they can reflect on what they are saying and deepen their faith. If you use some of them with your children at bedtime or before meals, you might also say them more slowly and thoughtfully.

The Sign of the Cross
In the name of the Father, and of the Son, and of the Holy Spirit. Amen.
(St Augustine also has a beautiful version of the Sign of the Cross: In the name of the Lover, and of the Beloved, and of the Spirit of Love between them. Amen.)

Our Father
Our Father, who art in heaven,
Hallowed be thy name.
Thy kingdom come;
Thy will be done on earth as it is in heaven.
Give us this day our daily bread,
And forgive us our trespasses,
As we forgive those who trespass against us,
And lead us not into temptation,
But deliver us from evil. Amen

Acts of Faith
You are the Christ, the Son of the living God.
My Lord and my God.
Lord, increase my faith.

Hail Mary
Hail Mary, full of grace,
The Lord is with you.
Blessed are you among women,
And blessed is the fruit of your womb, Jesus.
Holy Mary, Mother of God,
Pray for us sinners,
Now and at the hour of our death, Amen.

Morning Prayer
Father in heaven, you love me,
You're with me night and day.
I want to love you always in all I do and say.
I'll try to please you, Father.
Bless me through the day.
Amen.

Night Prayer
God our Father, I come to say
Thank you for your love today.
Thank you for my family
And all the friends you give to me.
Guard me in the dark of night and in the morning send your light. Amen.

Prayer for your family
Dear loving God, thank you for
my family with all the joys and
challenges they have brought
me. Help us to be one and holy
in our love for one another in
good times and bad times. Help
us to be flexible and firm, open
to different ways, open to our
neighbours and those in need.
We trust ourselves into the
hands of your Spirit – bless us
with your love and form us into
a little church in the Body of
your Son, Jesus Christ. Amen

Magnificat *(German version)*
My soul glorifies you, God, and
my spirit finds its joy in you,
my Saviour. For you have
blessed me lavishly and make
me ready to respond. You
shatter my little world and let
me be poor before you. You
take from me all my plans and
give me more than I can hope
for or ask or even imagine.
You give me opportunities and
the ability to be free and to burst
through my boundaries. You
give me the courage to be
daring, to trust in you alone, for
you show yourself as the ever-
greater one in my life. You
have taught me that it is in
being servant that it becomes
possible for me to allow God's
Kingdom to break through here
and now. Amen

Mysteries of the Rosary
Joyful Mysteries: The
Annunciation. The Visitation.
The birth of Jesus. The
Presentation in the Temple. The
Finding in the Temple.
Sorrowful Mysteries The Agony
in the Garden. The Scourging
at the Pillar. The Crowning
with thorns. The Carrying of
the Cross. The Crucifixion.
Glorious Mysteries. The
Resurrection. The Ascension.
The Coming of the Holy Spirit.
The Assumption of Mary into
Heaven. The Coronation.
Mysteries of light. The Baptism
of Jesus. The wedding feast of
Cana. The Proclaiming of the
Kingdom of God and Invitation
to Conversion. The
Transfiguration. The mystery
of the Eucharist.

Grace before Meals
Bless us, O Lord, as we sit
together. Bless the food we eat
today. Bless the hands that
made this meal. Bless us, o
Lord. Amen.

Aspirational Verses
My Lord and my God.
Jesus, have mercy on me a
sinner.
My God and my all.
You have made us for yourself,
Lord, and our hearts are restless
until they rest in you.

PAIDREACHA AS GAEILGE

An Phaidir
Ar nAthair atá ar neamh,
Go naofar d'ainm,
Go dtaga do ríocht,
Go ndéantar do thoil ar an
talamh mar a dhéantar ar
neamh.
Ar n-arán laethúil tabhair dúinn
inniu, Agus maith dúinn ár
bhfiacha, mar a mhaithimidne
dár bhféichiúna féin,
Agus ná lig sinn I gcathú,
Ach saor sinn ó olc. Amen.

Failte an Aingil
Sé do bheatha, a Mhuire,
Atá lán de ghrásta,
Tá an Tiarna leat.
Is beannaithe thú idir mná,
Agus is beannaithe toradh do
bhroinne, Iosa.
A Naomh Mhuire, a mháthair
Dé, Guigh orainn, na peacaigh,
Anois agus ar uair ár mbáis.
Amen.

Glóir don Athair
Glóir don Athair,
Agus don Mhac,
Agus don Spiorad Naomh;
Mar a bhí ó thús,
Mar atá anois,
Agus mar a bhéas go brách,
Le saol na saol.
Amen.

Altú roimh Bhia
Beannacht ó Dhia orainne atá ag
suí chun boird le chéile.
Beannacht ar an mbia a ithimid
inniu. Beannacht ar na lámha a
d'ullmhaigh dúinn é.
Beannacht ó Dhia dílis orainn
féin. Amen.

Altú i ndiaidh Bia
Go raibh maith agat, a Dhia,
mar is tú a thug bia dúinn.
Go raibh maith agat, a Dhia,
mar is tú a thug cairde dúinn.
Go rabih maith agat, a Dhia,
mar is tú a thug gach rud dúinn.
Go raibh maith agat, a Dhia.
Amen.

Paidir na Maidine
A Dhia, tá grá agat dom.
Bíonn tú liom de lá is d'oíche.
Ba mhaith liom grá a thabhairt
duit gach nóiméad den lá.
Ba mhaith liom tú a shásamh.
A athair, cabhraigh liom.
Amen.

Paidir na hOíche
A Dhia, a Athair, molaim thú
As ucht do chineáltais liom
inniu.
As ucht mo chairde molaim thú,
Agus as an teaghlach a thug tú
dom.
I ndorchadas na hoíche cosain
mé, solas na maidine go bhfeice
mé. Amen.

USING TWO CANDLES

We create a prayerful atmosphere of peace and calm when we light a candle as part of a grace before meals. There is a growing custom on many occasions of lighting *two* candles, one for the past and one for the future. New Year's Day (or Eve). The beginning of each new season. The end of a school term. The beginning or end of a holiday. The passing of an examination. A child leaving home. A birthday. An anniversary... As we light the candle for the past, we offer a prayer of thanks for the blessings linked with that occasion (and sometimes sorrow for our neglect). As we light the second candle, we might look to the future with a prayer trusting ourselves into God's hands – and perhaps asking for a new, more generous spirit.

There are also *times in the Church calendar* when we are encouraged to light a candle for the past we are leaving behind and a candle for the new season we are welcoming. All Souls' Day, Easter, Christmas, the beginning of Lent and Advent. For All Soul's Day, for example, we might light the candle for the past as we remember friends and family who have died – and the candle for the future as we pray *with* those souls that we will live more loving Christian lives.

For all these occasions we can change an ordinary meal into a celebration by having something like crisps and dip for a starter and an ice cream to finish – or something healthier! As far as the children are concerned, the meal itself may be much more important than the candle or the prayer, but faith is more likely to be 'caught' when it is linked with enjoyable times.

Here is a short reflection, based on a well-known scripture passage, which might sometimes be read before lighting the candles:

For everything there is a season and a time under heaven.
There is a time for sowing seeds and a time for gathering.
A time for Lent and a time for Easter.
A time for summer and a time for snow.
A time for school to start and a time for it to finish
A time for tears and a time for giving thanks
Let us take time, dear God, to celebrate you in all these times
of our lives together. Amen

APPENDIX 2: USING GUIDED MEDITATIONS WITH YOUR CHILDREN

INTRODUCTION

The purpose of the guided meditations below is to help children experience the presence of Jesus in scripture. (It is often overlooked that Jesus is present not only in the bread and wine at Mass but also in the Scriptures – and in the priest and people, the Body of Christ around us.)

These meditations have all been tried by parents with their children and it is now clear that this type of prayer certainly satisfies a hunger in many young people. Don't think of them as something to be used only once. The same meditation can be used a number of times and the children's experience of it will tend to be different each time.

When to use them

It will generally help to try doing a meditation on your own first: you should then feel more confident in introducing it to your children.

There is no set time to ease a young person into praying with scripture like this, but you may like to try one of these meditations for 'family prayer' at a weekend. Or when a child is ill some Sunday, you might say, "You're obviously feeling too unwell to go to church today. We'll have a guided meditation instead. That will be easier for you."

There is something to be said for starting with just one child, as the presence of another can change the atmosphere – sitting in silence in the presence of each other can sometimes cause giggling. But once a family is used to this form of prayer they relax and the presence of a number of people can actually add to the experience.

How they work

Each meditation begins with a short period of quietening down followed by the lighting of a candle as a sign of the presence of Christ (the Light of the World) where two or more are praying together. It may help to put a marker at the 'Quietening Down' page below (p. 60) and at the passage you have chosen. Very soft background music can be played throughout the quietening time – and through the entire meditation – because music often creates a better atmosphere for prayer, especially if people are not comfortable with silence.

After the quietening down exercise, you slowly read the guided meditation you have chosen, pausing briefly where pauses are shown. The suggested times are for families who are not used to praying like this – ideally you would need a longer silence. It would be normal to extend times of silence as your children get *used* to them – and if they seem ready for that.

Finally, everyone opens their eyes again and you can ask your child(ren) some of the suggested questions below that you think are suitable. This sharing of what happened for each one can add to and deepen the prayer experience.

The suggested sequence, then, is:
1. Read the 'quietening down' exercise and light a candle.
2. Slowly read the passage and script that follows it.
3. Ask some of the suggested questions

Making up your own meditations
When you have led your children through a number of meditations with scripture, you might consider making up your own meditations. Pray to the Spirit to help you, then choose a passage of scripture and try praying with it yourself first, using your imagination to recreate the scene. Remember that **the goal is not to sort out your problems but to meet Jesus** – keep focused on that. (A simple book on praying with scripture is "Enjoy Praying," available from Family Caring Trust, Ashtree Enterprise Park, Newry BT34 1BY. It costs £7.95/€10.80 including postage and packing.) After praying on a passage, you might then make a few notes to help you introduce the passage to your children. You can use the same quietening exercises as are in this book, and similar questions for afterwards.

Checklist
This book – with markers at the right pages.
CD of reflective instrumental music.
CD player.
A candle
Matches.
A reading light (if you are reading these notes in semi-darkness – which may help to create a better atmosphere and cut down on distractions).

QUIETENING DOWN

The following passage can be read with only short pauses before each meditation, but feel free to change it or leave it out as you think fit.
First, we'll take a moment to calm ourselves. It's good to keep your back straight, put your feet on the ground, close your eyes, and take a little while to still yourself first. Try to breathe through your nose and become aware of the cool breath as it enters through your nose.. (pause) and the warm breath as you breathe out.. (pause).

The Holy Spirit is within each of us. So relax and soften your body to let the Spirit flow through you... Your feet first, don't move them, but let a soft feeling flow through them as you become aware of your toes.. the soles of your feet.. your heels.. your ankles... Let that softness flow up through your legs into your knees – let the tension go in your knees.. your thighs.. your stomach.. your lower back.. your waist.. Now the entire lower part of your body... Get away from the thoughts that buzz through your mind, and just be aware of your body, because we can shut God out when we don't have some silence and some body-awareness in our lives.

And now let the Spirit move through the upper part of your body as you let that softness and relaxation move through your upper back... your chest... your shoulders. Let the tension in your shoulders go. And now soften your neck... and the back of your head... the top of your head... your face. Notice the tension in your jaws and chin as you let it go... Back to your shoulders now... and down your upper arms into your elbows... your forearms... your wrists.. your hands.. your fingers and thumbs. Now relax your whole body and mind, and let the Spirit of Peace flow through you as you come more fully into the presence of God.

(Lighting candle) Jesus, where two or more are gathered in your name, you said you would be in our midst, so we believe you are present now. We ask the Holy Spirit to help us meet you as the passage is read... (Pause. Then read chosen passage - see page 61-74.)

QUESTIONS AFTER THE MEDITATION

You can open your eyes now and come back gradually to the room. Was the quietening time too long or too short? Was it hard to imagine the scene? What did you see that filled in the scene for you? Were you able to put *yourself* into the story? Were you able to meet Jesus? How do you feel now at the end of the meditation?

JESUS IN THE UPPER ROOM
John 20, 19-22

Many of us think of the Gospel stories as events that happened two thousand years ago. We can easily miss the point that Jesus is present right here and now whenever the Gospel is read. The passage we're going to listen to is about Jesus appearing to his friends in the upper room. <u>You</u> are one of his friends and you can meet him and be with him now as the passage is read:

When it was evening on that day, the first day of the week, and the doors of the house where the disciples had met were locked for fear of the Jews, Jesus came and stood among them and said, "Peace be with you." After he said this, he showed them his hands and his side. Then the disciples rejoiced when they saw the Lord. Jesus said to them again, "Peace be with you. As the Father has sent me, so I send you." When he had said this, he breathed on them and said to them, "Receive the Holy Spirit." (John 20, 19-22)

We'll take the first part again. *It was evening on that day, the first day of the week, and the doors of the house where the disciples had met were locked for fear of the Jews.* I wonder can you imagine that *you* are in the upper room where the disciples are. Look around in your mind's eye and see the rough white walls... (pause for 3-4 seconds.) Notice the big wooden door – firmly closed with wooden bars across it, blocking the way in... (3-4 secs) Look around at the disciples now and see the fear in their eyes – they're wondering if they're going to be attacked next... (3-4 secs) It might be good to ask yourself what <u>your</u> fears are – for yourself or family or friends? What are <u>you</u> most afraid of in life...? (5 secs) Pray for the grace to see what fears are blocking you from letting Jesus in... (5 secs)

We'll continue with the reading: *Jesus came and stood among them and said, "Peace be with you." After he said this, he showed them his hands and his side.* So become aware now of the presence of Jesus. Sense his presence... (3-4 secs) Look at his hands and see the wounds... (3-4 secs) Remember that he is really present – it's not just something we're imagining. Even if you can't see his face, hear him speak, let him say your name, and let him say to you personally, "Peace be with you..." (pause for 5-10 seconds)

And we'll continue again with the reading: *Then the disciples rejoiced when they saw the Lord. Jesus said to them again, "Peace be with you. As the Father has sent me, so I send you." When he had said*

61

this, he breathed on them and said to them "Receive the Holy Spirit."
Let Jesus speak to you personally now: I'm saying *peace be with you*
a second time, he says, because I so much want peace for you and for
your family and friends... (3-4 secs) Peace... (3-4 secs) Trust in
me, don't worry about anything – life may be difficult at times, but I
will always be with you, loving you... (3-4 secs) Trust in me and be
at peace... (3-4 secs) As the Father sent me, so I send you to bring
my peace and love and joy to others, to your family, to all you meet...
(3-4 secs) So I breathe on you now and say: Receive the Holy Spirit.
(3-4 secs) Receive the Holy Spirit for yourself and your family, and
be at peace... (3-4 secs) I have given you my Spirit in Baptism and I
give it more fully in Confirmation, and I will continue to give you my
Spirit of Love as long as you live. (5-10 secs) You may like to take a
moment to thank God for the great gift of the Spirit. (5-10 secs)
You can open your eyes now and come back gradually to the room...

THE COMING OF THE HOLY SPIRIT AT PENTECOST
Acts 2, 1-4
You remember that Jesus had promised a powerful filling with the
Holy Spirit, so the apostles and Mary and others had been praying
and preparing for this gift for some time. Here's the story of
Pentecost from the first reading for Pentecost Sunday:
*When the day of Pentecost had come, they were all together in one place.
And suddenly from heaven there came a sound like the rush of a violent
wind, and it filled the entire house where they were sitting. Divided
tongues, as of fire, appeared among them, and a tongue rested on each
of them. All of them were filled with the Holy Spirit and began to speak
in other languages, as the Spirit gave them ability.*

Now we'll take the passage bit by bit, remembering that what is
described when Scripture is read happens again for anyone with an
open heart. (brief pause) *When the day of Pentecost had come, they
were all together in one place. And suddenly from heaven there came a
sound like the rush of a violent wind, and it filled the entire house where
they were sitting.*

You may like to put yourself in the room with the disciples now
and to pray for the grace to be open to receive the Spirit... (5 secs)
Can you imagine now the sound of this powerful wind, like a great
tornado or whirlwind...? (brief pause) That can give us an idea of
how much we are loved – St John of the Cross says that God rushes

like a powerful whirlwind into any heart that is open. And that whirlwind of love is here now, rushing in to fill our hearts when we empty them of the wants and desires that usually fill them, and when we come humbly before God to admit our emptiness and weakness... (2-3 secs) Allow that whirlwind of love to enter into your heart now... (5-10 secs)

And we'll take the next line now. *Divided tongues, as of fire, appeared among them, and a tongue rested on each of them.* Can you imagine that – fire entering the room? Fire is something a bit scary. It hurts. It burns. And when we open ourselves to love, that's what happens, it hurts to love, to go against what we <u>feel</u> like doing out of love... (brief pause) The fire separates now and comes to rest on the head of each one in the room. Are you ready for this fire of love that will burn you? When you're ready, invite the Spirit, who is a flame of love, into your heart... (10 secs)

And now the next line. *All of them were filled with the Holy Spirit and began to speak in other languages, as the Spirit gave them ability.* We don't know how many languages the apostles spoke when the Spirit filled them. But we do know that there's one language everyone understands – the language of love. And the same passage goes on to tell us about the extraordinary love shown by the early Christians after receiving the Spirit. That's the proof that the Spirit is alive and active in us – that we love one another – in what we think about people, what we say about people, and how we treat them. So we might ask the Spirit now for the grace to be kinder and more loving at home, at work, at school, wherever. Ask for that grace and it will certainly be given. (5 secs) And relax now and allow the Holy Spirit of Love to flow into your heart. (10 secs)

As usual before we finish a time of prayer, we might take a few moments to say thanks. Whether you sensed the presence of the Spirit or not, there is no doubt that the Spirit was present, blessing you and your family. (brief pause) You can open your eyes now and come back in your own time to the room we're in...

CURE OF THE BLIND MAN
(Mark 8 22-26)

They came to Bethsaida. Some people brought a blind man to him and begged him to touch him. He took the blind man by the hand and led him out of the village; and when he had put saliva on his eyes and laid his hands on him, he asked him, "Can you see anything?" And the man looked up and said, "I can see people, but they look like trees, walking." Then Jesus laid his hands on his eyes again: and he looked intently and his sight was restored, and he saw everything clearly. Then he sent him away to his home, saying, "Do not even go into the village."

We'll take the first part. *They came to Bethsaida. Some people brought a blind man to him and begged him to touch him.* (pause) **So we'll start by imagining that we happen to be in the little village of Bethsaida that day... It's a poor village, with hot, dusty streets, no footpaths, just a dirt path – can you imagine that?** (3-4 secs) **And now see the blind beggar being taken round the corner to meet Jesus. Can you see the old ragged clothes the man is wearing?** (3-4 secs) **Look at Jesus' face as they bring the blind man to him – what feelings can you see in his eyes...?** (5 secs)

Now, remember that what happened in the gospels is happening right here at this present moment. You are no longer an observer outside the scene. You are the blind person. After all, there are many ways in which we are blind. We can be blind to the most important things in life when we don't take time to see God in our lives or in the people we meet. So take a moment to become aware of some ways in which you are blind... (about 5 secs)

You've been brought now into the presence of Jesus. He is really present to you at this moment. Feel the sense of privilege to be here, and tell him about your own blindness... (5-10 secs)

And back to the passage. *He took the blind man by the hand and led him out of the village.* **Jesus also wants to lead** *you* **away from what you're used to, to lead you to a different place... Are you prepared to let him lead you?...** (5 secs)

When he had put saliva on his eyes and laid his hands on him, he asked him, "Can you see anything?" And the man looked up and said, "I can see people, but they look like trees, walking." **Let Jesus rub the saliva on your blindness, and sense how much he loves you as he touches you...** (2-3 secs) **Pray for healing so that you may no longer be blind but may see Christ in your family and in your friends and in everyone you meet** (2-3 secs)

Now you begin to see, but it's blurred. Changing the way you see people is going to take time. Ask Jesus to touch you again and again so that you will be able to see with eyes of faith and love... (pause)

Then Jesus laid his hands on his eyes again: and he looked intently and his sight was restored, and he saw everything clearly. (pause) **Now Jesus lays his hands on your eyes again. Sense the great power of God that flows through him to heal your blindness...** (pause) **And you begin to see more clearly. Like the blind man, the first thing you see is Jesus himself. Talk to him in your own words and say to him whatever you want to say to him...** (5-10 secs) **And now listen to what he wants to say to you...** (5-10 secs)

Then he sent him away to his home, saying, "Do not even go into the village." **Jesus is asking you not to go backwards. Not to go back to the blindness, to your old ways of looking at things. Talk with him about that...** (5 secs)

And you may like to take a moment to thank him... (5 secs) **You can open your eyes and come back in your own time to the room...**

JESUS CALMS THE STORM
(Matthew 8 23-27)

The passage we're going to pray on now is about Jesus calming the storm, so it's good to remember that Jesus is present here with us, bringing us peace and calm just as he does in the story.

And when he got into the boat, his disciples followed him. A gale arose on the lake, so great that the boat was being swamped by the waves; but he was asleep. And they went and woke him up saying, 'Lord, save us! We are perishing!' And he said to them, 'Why are you afraid, you of little faith?' Then he got up and rebuked the winds and the sea; and there was a dead calm. They were amazed, saying, 'What sort of man is this, that even the winds and the sea obey him?' (Matthew 8 23-27)

We'll start with the first line of the story: *And when Jesus got into the boat, his disciples followed him.*

Can you see the beautiful lake of Galilee in your mind's eye, with the mountains rising up behind in the distance... See the blue sky? (2-3 secs) **Listen to the birds singing and the water lapping...** (3 secs) **Now see Jesus walking down to where the boat is tied. He's looking tired – he was up this morning before dawn to pray.** (3 secs) **The disciples climb into the boat behind him, and you are invited now to get in with them too...** (3 secs) **And the boat pushes out to sea. Jesus stretches out in the back of the boat and falls asleep quickly. Look at the peace of his sleeping face, and let some of his peace and trust in God into your own heart...** (5-6 secs)

*A gale arose on the lake, so great that the boat was being swamped by
the waves; but he was asleep. And they went and woke him up saying,
'Lord, save us! We are perishing!'* It might be good to ask yourself
what the storm is in your own life. For some of us, it may be just the
hectic pace of life today, with too much to do, always on the go,
feeling we can't cope. We could easily say with the disciples, "Lord,
help us – we are perishing." Or it may be something that's worrying
you or upsetting you. Some of us may have worries about money, or
school, or exams... Or it may be something that we'd find hard to
talk to anyone about... Or it may be some difficulty about friends
that's upsetting us... Ask the Holy Spirit to help you see what the
storm in your life is...? (5-6 secs) So often, when we meet a problem,
we panic like these disciples. We forget to have faith and to trust
that we're in God's hands. So turn to Jesus now who is present to
you at this moment just as he was with the disciples that day in the
boat... Tell him about your worries, your storm – don't keep it to
yourself. (5 secs) And don't be afraid to tell him how weak you are:
you might repeat a number of times like the disciples, "Lord, help
me! I'm perishing! Lord, help us! We're perishing!" (5-10 secs)
*And he said to them, 'Why are you afraid, you of little faith?' Then
he got up and rebuked the winds and the sea; and there was a dead
calm.* Listen to what Jesus says to you: "Why are you so afraid, you
of little faith? Why don't you trust me more? Why don't you turn
to me instead of trying to deal with your worries and problems on
your own..." (3 secs) Try to hand over your fears and worries now
into God's hands – let Jesus calm the storm inside you... (5-10 secs)
*They were amazed, saying, 'What sort of man is this, that even the
winds and the sea obey him?'* Let yourself feel some of their
astonishment and wonder and thanks in the loving presence of
God... (3 secs) So we finish by thanking God for the hope and the
love and the peace of the Holy Spirit that has certainly been given to
us, whether we feel it or not. (5 secs) When you're ready you can
come back gently to the room, and open your eyes...

HEALING OF THE PARALYSED MAN
(Mark 2, 1-12)
We'll look today at the cure of the man who was paralysed. Can you
tell me first what it means to be paralysed...? Okay, you remember
this man had good friends who wanted to do all they could to help

him, so when they found the house thronged where Jesus was, they got up on the roof, took off the tiles and lowered him down. Jesus was impressed with their faith. But he said something that surprised and disappointed them. The man wanted a cure, and all Jesus said to him was, "Your sins are forgiven." (pause)

Jesus said that for a reason. He is drawing attention to a deeper kind of paralysis that affects many people like you and me. Spiritual paralysis. Where we're not able to move forward in our lives or to grow as loving persons. We become spiritually paralysed because we have got into habits in our lives that stop us from becoming more loving. So a good starting place for our prayer now is to ask ourselves where we are paralysed or stuck, and not becoming more loving. Ask the Holy Spirit for the grace to see where you are stuck spiritually, because recognising that is a first step to healing... (5-10 secs)

Now, the paralysed man had friends to bring him to Jesus, and we could also be doing with some friends to bring us into the presence of Jesus. People like his mother Mary, your favourite saints, also people who have died who love you (like granny/ granddad). Ask them to draw you into the presence of God and lower you, as it were, down from the roof into the presence of Jesus... (4-5 secs) Let Jesus look at you now and listen to him as he says, "I can see that you are paralysed... But your lack of love is forgiven... I'm going to give you the strength, if you want it, to live a more loving life..." Talk with him about what you want... (about 10 secs)

Let God's grace touch you now, and feel the strength come into your body and your spirit. Speak to Jesus and talk about what you'd like to do with your life now... (5-10 secs)

And we'll take a moment to thank God for the graces of this prayer... (5-10 secs) You can open your eyes now and bring yourself gently back to the room.

RAISING OF THE WIDOW'S SON
(Luke 7, 11-17)

Soon afterwards he went to a town called Nain and his disciples and a large crowd went with him. As he approached the gate of the town, a man who had died was being carried out. He was his mother's only son and she was a widow; and with her was a large crowd from the town.

When the Lord saw her, he had compassion for her and said to her, "Do not weep." Then he came up and touched the bier and the bearers stood still. And he said, "Young man, I say to you, rise." The dead man sat up and began to speak, and Jesus gave him to his mother. Fear seized all of them and they glorified God, saying, "A great prophet has appeared among us!" and "God has looked favourably on his people."

We remember as we start that Jesus is here with us now, working the same miracles of grace in us as in the story. You may like to join the crowd close to Jesus and watch what happens... (3 secs)

When the Lord saw her, he had compassion for her and said to her, "Do not weep." Then he came up and touched the bier and the bearers stood still. And he said, "Young man, I say to you, rise." The dead man sat up and began to speak, and Jesus gave him to his mother. Notice that Jesus performed the miracle because he had *compassion* for her." Look at his face and see the love in his eyes. (4-5 secs) See him touching the funeral stand... And everyone is astonished to hear him say with authority in his voice, "Young man, I say to you, rise." (4-5 secs)

Jesus is present with us at this moment. He has the same love and understanding and pity for us, and all those we care for, as he had for the widow. See the compassion and love in his eyes as he speaks to you now... He says, "I can see the deadness in you and I want to offer you hope and new life just as I did then..." He puts his hands on you and says, '(John/Sarah – say your children's name), I say to you, rise." What does he mean? Let him tell you himself. (5-10 secs)

Jesus wants to bring healing and new life and hope to you and all your friends and your family. Take a few moments to pray also for them, remembering that we're praying together in his name, so our prayers are very powerful and healing for them. (10 secs)

And we continue with the passage, *Fear seized all of them and they glorified God, saying, "A great prophet has appeared among us!" and "God has looked favourably on his people."* Note how astonished and delighted the crowd is, and how they did what we sometimes forget to do when we have been blessed – they praised and glorified God. So we might also take a moment to thank God for the hope and the love and the new life that God has just given to us and to the people we prayed for, whether we were aware of it or not... (4-5 secs)

And when you're ready you can come back gently to the room we're in, and open your eyes...

CALLING THE DISCIPLES
(Mark, 1 16-18)

Most of us have our heroes. We read about them and talk about them, and we often want to be more like them. It's not always pop-stars or footballers, though. It may be a parent, a teacher, a coach, a priest, a neighbour, a grandparent, an aunt, or a friend of the family. Some one who makes you feel special and you feel good when you're with them because you know they've time for you and they like you, the vibes are good. And because you're open to them, you usually learn more from them than from anyone else. Which makes you a disciple. Disciples are just people who learn from someone else because of the deep respect they have for that person.

If you had lived at the time of Jesus, he might very well have been a hero for you. Someone you would like to meet, and to listen to with extra interest. And the wonderful thing is that when the gospel is read, we do meet, not just a person who lived long ago – we actually meet Jesus here and now. Let's try that for ourselves.

As Jesus passed along the Sea of Galilee, he saw Simon and his brother Andrew casting a net into the lake – for they were fishermen. And Jesus said to them, "Follow me and I will make you fish for people." And immediately they left their nets and followed him.

Can you relax and put yourself into this scene. Sit on a stone near the water and see the blue sky... (2-3 secs) See the fishermen lowering their nets into the water... (2-3 secs) Now a lone figure appears, the person everyone has been talking about – who heals people, who cares for the poor, who speaks with authority... As you watch him come closer, you feel a great reverence and a sense of privilege to be in his presence... (5-10 secs)

And Jesus said to them, "Follow me and I will make you fish for people." And immediately they left their nets and followed him. Jesus stops near to where the boat is. The men pause from their work. They can hardly believe their ears. He's asking them to join him, to follow him. This is crazy. People who work with animals or fish were considered uncouth and sinful at the time. And here he is asking *them* to join him, to follow him. Them!

People in a family business don't easily drop everything and go off after a wandering preacher. But Simon and Andrew have no hesitation: this guy is different. They don't have to think about it. They feel privileged to be chosen. And they follow him. But now comes the crunch. Jesus turns around to you. He looks at you with deep, warm eyes. Can you see his eyes...? (5 secs) And he asks the same question of you – will you also become one of my disciples and follow me? Think about it before you answer, because it's not easy to drop your nets and decide, "This is it. This is someone I want to follow to the end." Following him will mean listening to what he says, stopping when I have to make a decision and asking him, "What's the most loving thing to do here, Jesus?" Talk for a minute or two with him, tell him your difficulty with what he's asking. Hear what he says. (10 secs)

If you can't decide, don't worry. Jesus accepts you just as you are. He offers: he doesn't push. He loves us just as much whether we decide to follow him or not. So take a moment to thank him now as we finish our meditation. (10 secs)

A meditation like this is not long enough to deal with the invitation to be a disciple. So you may like to take some time in the next few days to talk further with Jesus about your fears and what holds you back from being a disciple – maybe at night before you fall asleep. Remember, you can pray anytime. When you're ready now, you can open your eyes and come back gently to the room...

HEALING THE MAN WITH THE UNCLEAN SPIRIT
Mark 1 23-26

Just then there was in their synagogue a man with an unclean spirit, and he cried out, 'what have you to do with us, Jesus of Nazareth? Have you come to destroy us? I know who you are, the Holy One of God.' But Jesus rebuked him, saying, 'Be silent, and come out of him!' And the unclean spirit, throwing him into convulsions and crying with a loud voice, came out of him.

Let's take the first section; *Just then there was in their synagogue a man with an unclean spirit.* To meet the Jesus who is present here and now, it usually helps to get in touch with ourselves first. I need to think about the unclean spirit in myself. For there is a kind of unclean spirit in each one of us. It's a spirit that is negative, full of fears. It's the spirit that makes me feel inferior and insecure and makes me dislike myself. And when we hate ourselves, we usually find that we hate others too, we're critical of them, we look down on them. So let's take a minute in silence to be humble before God and get in touch with that unclean spirit in ourselves. (10-15 secs)

And the next line. *And he cried out, 'what have you to do with us, Jesus of Nazareth? Have you come to destroy us? I know who you are, the Holy One of God.* An unclean spirit is very uncomfortable in the presence of love. It fights love. It cannot exist side by side with love. It rightly says to Jesus, 'Have you come to destroy us?' So let's come now into the presence of Jesus, burdened by this nasty spirit within us, and ask humbly for help. (5-10 secs)

Jesus, you are the most loving person who ever walked the earth, you are the Holy One of God. We come humbly before you, burdened by our negative, unloving thoughts. We are in great need of healing so that we can really love those we meet each day. Have pity on us please... (3-4 secs)

And the last line: *But Jesus rebuked him, saying, 'Be silent, and come out of him!' And the unclean spirit, throwing him into convulsions and crying with a loud voice, came out of him.* Look at Jesus now. He is the exact opposite of this nasty spirit within us – strong, loving, full of goodness. (5 secs) But there is a stern look in his face in the presence of evil. He speaks with authority. He says to that nasty, proud, spiteful spirit in each of us, 'Be silent, and come out of him. Be silent, and come out of her. Stop that negative, critical whispering within, be off with you, let my beloved people alone, let them grow in love.' Let him say that now to the unclean spirit within you (5-10 secs).

You are in the real presence of Jesus now. Allow that healing presence to touch you, to enter deep into your soul and to melt away your negative, critical spirit... Sense the healing power of God within you... (about 10 secs)

God often allows an unclean spirit to remain with us to keep us humble, so it may remain with you, but the difference is that you have now been given the grace to *control* that spirit instead of letting it control you. So let's take a moment to join with Jesus in thanking our Father for healing us. For there has been a real healing of spirit for us, whether we are aware of it or not. (5-10 secs) Dear God, you are Father and Mother of us all, and you love us more than we can imagine. With Jesus and through Jesus we thank you for the power to overcome the unclean spirit within us. Amen. (pause)

And when you're ready you can come back gently to the room we're in...

JESUS COMES TO SIMON'S HOME
(Mark 1, 29-31

As soon as they left the synagogue, they entered the house of Simon and Andrew, with James and John. Now, Simon's mother-in-law was in bed with a fever, and they told him about her at once. He came and took her by the hand, and lifted her up. Then the fever left her, and she began to serve them.

We'll begin with the first section. *As soon as they left the synagogue, they entered the house of Simon and Andrew, with James and John.* Can you imagine how Simon and Andrew felt? They had just left their nets to follow this extraordinary person, Jesus – and now he comes to stay in their home. (pause) How would you feel if you could have Jesus come to stay in this house? (pause) And you can! When you welcome a visitor, a neighbour, a school friend, a relative into your home, you welcome Jesus. Or if you do any act of kindness, a chore for someone in your home, or take time to listen and chat to another member of your family, you are welcoming Jesus into your home. Take a moment to thank him for that privilege and to ask for greater faith, the eyes to see him in others. (8-10 secs)

And the next line. *Now, Simon's mother-in-law was in bed with a fever, and they told him about her at once.* This is the lovely thing about welcoming Jesus in your home – you always get more than you give. His is a healing presence, and when you are open to him you too will be healed. But you don't have to be physically ill to be healed. We need healing in all sorts of ways, so let Jesus come to you now as he came to Simon's mother-in-law. He sits down beside you, present to you, interested in you. Can you sense his presence? (2-3 secs) Now he asks you what healing you need. Do you need to be healed of your difficulty in forgiving someone, or a habit of showing off, or saying nasty things to or about someone else? Tell Jesus in your own words about your difficulty. If you ask for his healing, you will certainly get it. Take your time to talk with him. (10-20 secs)

He came and took her by the hand, and lifted her up. Then the fever left her, and she began to serve them. Let Jesus take you by the hand too, and lift *you* up. (pause) Sense the healing in his touch and let him tell you how he is healing you. (5 secs) But notice something important here – 'then the fever left her, and she began to *serve* them.' Jesus heals us because he loves us – no strings attached – but

72

the real healing and strength comes when we serve others. That's when your healing becomes true healing. So maybe you'd like to make some resolution now to move out of yourself and think of the needs of someone else. Decide what you'll do. (5 seconds) And you might end as usual by taking a moment to thank Jesus in your own words for being a guest in your home, and for his healing. (5-10 secs) And when you're ready you can open your eyes and come back gently to the room we're in...

JESUS CLEANSES A LEPER
(Mark 1, 40-42)

We pray to meet Jesus now as St Mark describes how he healed a leper. *A leper came to him begging him, and kneeling he said to him, 'If you choose, you can make me clean.' Moved with pity, Jesus stretched out his hand and touched him and said to him, 'I do choose. Be made clean!' Immediately the leprosy left him and he was made clean.*

Let's take it a little at a time. *A leper came to him begging him, and kneeling he said to him, 'If you choose, you can make me clean.'* This story isn't just about a leper who lived two thousand years ago. Leprosy in the Bible is a symbol for sin, and we are all sinners – we are all people who sin in the way we treat others or think about others or talk about others – that is our leprosy before God. So let's begin by asking God to help us to see the ways *we* are suffering from the leprosy of sin in how we fail to respect others... (5 secs)

And we'll think now about what it's like to be a leper. We can easily forget that this leper would have been a normal person before he picked up the disease. He may have been a popular person in his village. He may have been deeply loved by his wife and children. But as soon as he was diagnosed, there wasn't even a chance to say goodbye, he had to go immediately and live as an outcast. And that is also what sin does – it cuts us off, it makes us outcasts and condemns us like lepers to a hopeless fate. So let's pray for the grace to know how awful sin is, how awful our lack of love is... (5-10 secs)

Yet this leper had one desperate hope left. He had heard of Jesus as a healer, so he went to meet him. And he had great faith, 'If you choose,' he said, ' you can make me clean.' (brief pause) You might like to kneel alongside the leper now as he meets Jesus. (brief pause) And with the leper ask Jesus for his help, perhaps asking with the same words, 'If you choose, you can make me clean.' (5-10 secs.)

Now the next line. *Moved with pity, Jesus stretched out his hand and touched him and said to him, 'I do choose. Be made clean!' Immediately the leprosy left him and he was made clean.*

'Moved with pity.' See the compassion and sadness in Jesus' eyes as he looks at the poor man and understands his pain and isolation... (3-4 secs) And now let him turn his eyes to you with the same compassion and understanding.. (5 secs) And let him say to you, 'I do choose. Be made clean!' (5 secs)

You are in the presence of Jesus now – it is not just your imagination. He is truly present, healing you. Let his warmth and healing and forgiveness spread through your body, forgiving you for the disrespect you have shown others in your thoughts and words and actions. (5-10 secs)

Part of any healing from sin is to turn over a new leaf and resolve not to sin again, so take a moment for that and to ask for that grace. (5 secs)

Be at peace now and thank Jesus for his love and caring for yourself and for everyone in need. (5-10 secs)

And when you're ready you can come back gently to the room we're in and open your eyes...

A RITUAL MEAL AT HOME

Praying on the Scripture passages above can help a family to begin to experience the presence of Jesus in the first part of Mass. A ritual meal can be a good way to help children understand what happens in the second half of Mass. Indeed, Tad Guzie, in his book, *Jesus and the Eucharist* states that "religious educators have found that if they can talk people into making one meal a week a real family meal, a ritual meal with a blessing and a sharing of thanks, and a cup passed around the table, teaching about the Eucharist becomes easy sailing." Below is an outline that may help to introduce that.

Checklist: A glass of water and a bowl, a glass of wine or grape juice, a tissue, a twig or thin stick, a small fresh roll of French bread on a plate.

Parent speaking: **We sometimes hear of people who are willing to give their life for others. We might think that means to die for them. But it doesn't usually mean that. Giving your life for others is what many people do – they give their time and money and energy day in and day out and wear themselves out for their families. That's giving your life for others. That's what Jesus asks us to do for others.**

That's what he did. At the Last Supper, he could have lifted a small twig and said, 'You see this twig? It's my body, and look' (breaking it in small pieces) **'it's going to be broken and given up for all the people I love. Take a piece each to keep in memory of me.' And he could have taken water and said, 'Look. You see this water? This is my blood that's going to be spilled for you.** (spilling the water into a bowl to illustrate). **And when I say** *Do this in memory of me,* **what I'm really asking you is to be willing to do the same as me – to give your life for others. Not to** *die* **for them, but to** *live in love* **for them. He could have said and done that.**

But Jesus didn't do that. He went further. He didn't take water and a piece of wood. First he took a loaf of the ordinary bread at the time. He said, 'Look, you see this? This is my body.' He broke it as a sign that his body would be broken for us. (breaking it) **But then he handed it out and said, "Eat it. You will be my Body in future. And this bread will strengthen you and make you able to give your life away like me."** (giving it out.)

Then he took the fruit of the grape, which is much richer than water, and he said, 'This is my blood that's going to be spilled for you.' But he didn't spill it into a bowl. He gave it to them and said, "Drink this. I'm giving my life to you now – you will be my Body and Blood in future. It will strengthen you and make you able to love like me." (Passing it around with a tissue.)

What you have just eaten and drunk, of course, is ordinary bread and grape juice. Doing what we have just done may help us to understand better what Jesus was doing, but it's obviously not the same as joining people for Communion at Mass. That's why we go to Mass.

RESOURCES

BOOKS

There is a series of booklets for parents published by Veritas entitled: **Will our children be okay?** Each one costs around £4-5 stg/€6-7. The titles and authors are: **Will our Children Believe?** by Michael Paul Gallagher SJ **Will our Children have Family Prayer?** by Clare Maloney **How will our Children Grow?** by Christy Kenneally **Your Child and Drugs** by Sean Cassin **Children Feeling Good** by Tony Humphreys **Will our Children Build Healthy Relationships?** by Angela McNamara **Helping your Child through Bereavement** by Mary Paula Walsh **When Parents Separate: Helping your Children Cope** by John Sharry, Peter Reid and Eugene Donohue **Bringing up Responsible Children** by John Sharry **Bringing up Responsible Teenagers** by John Sharry. Or see www.veritas.ie

Enjoy Praying, by Michael and Terri Quinn is a simple introduction to meeting and getting to know Jesus as you pray with Scripture. Available from Family Caring Trust, 8 Ashtree Enterprise Park, Newry, Co. Down BT34 1BY (£7.95/€10.80, incl. post and packing.) Books on parenting by Michael and Terri (each the same price as above) include '**From Pram to Primary School,' 'What can a Parent do?' 'What can the parent of a teenager do?' Parenting and Sex'** and '**Being Assertive.**' For books and ideas on parenting see www.familycaring.co.uk

Any book by parent and educator Dr Kathleen O'Connell Chesto tends to be fresh and up to date in helping us see the sacred in the ordinary. A good example is **Raising Kids Who Care**, published Sheed and Ward, ISBN 1 55612 921 1. Also **At home with our faith**. And **Growing faith, growing family.**

A book that may be helpful in getting to know the real Jesus is **Jesus before Christianity** (Orbis), by Albert Nolan, ISBN 1570754047.

WEBSITES

www.homefaith.com – practical ideas to develop family spirituality.
www.couples-place.com and www.marriagetools.com sites dedicated to marriage and building relationships.
www.screenit.com – media reviews of latest films and videos

MAKING AGREEMENTS

At the beginning of a course, it can help to discuss and agree on the following guidelines – or any other concerns you may have.

Play your part. Some of us are naturally shy and reluctant to speak, even in a small group, so no one at any stage *has* to talk in the group. That said, the more you can take part the better – talking things out can help others as well as yourself.

Give the others a chance. If you talk too much, you may spoil things for others. Please don't speak a second time until others have at least had a chance to speak once. Better still if you can encourage others to talk first.

What works for you. The aim of this course is to help you to think and plan for yourself, so you are not expected to follow suggestions or agree with everything in the book – we are all different. But you are asked to give new ideas a fair chance by trying them out.

Keep it to yourself. It is important not to talk outside the group about anything that is said in the group – things can sound quite different when they are spoken about out of context.

What works for others. Please do not offer anyone advice. People have a right to their own approach and their own opinion. Feel free to say what works for you, but that may not work for others, and it is just not helpful to tell others what you think *they* ought to do. In the same spirit of respect, the group leaders will not offer advice either.